JACKIE ROBINSON

"All I Ask Is That You Respect Me as a Human Being"

Carin T. Ford

Series Consultant:
Dr. Russell L. Adams, Chairman
Department of
Afro-American Studies,
Howard University

Enslow Publishers, Inc.

40 Industrial Road   PO Box 38
Box 398   Aldershot
Berkeley Heights, NJ 07922   Hants GU12 6BP
USA   UK

http://www.enslow.com

"I'M NOT CONCERNED WITH YOUR LIKING
OR DISLIKING ME. . . . ALL I ASK IS THAT YOU
RESPECT ME AS A HUMAN BEING."

—*Jackie Robinson*

Copyright © 2005 by Carin T. Ford

All rights reserved.

No part of this book may be reproduced by any means
without the written permission of the publisher.

Library of Congress Cataloging-in-Publication Data

Ford, Carin T.
    Jackie Robinson : "all I ask is that you respect me as a human being" / Carin T. Ford.
       p. cm. — (African-American biography library)
    Includes bibliographical references and index.
    ISBN 0-7660-2461-X (hardcover)
    1. Robinson, Jackie, 1919–1972—Juvenile literature. 2. Baseball players—United
States—Biography—Juvenile literature. I. Title. II. Series.
    GV865.R6F67 2005
    796.357'092—dc22

                                                                    2004016798

Printed in the United States of America

10 9 8 7 6 5 4 3 2 1

To Our Readers:
We have done our best to make sure all Internet Addresses in this book were active and appro-
priate when we went to press. However, the author and the publisher have no control over and
assume no liability for the material available on those Internet sites or on other Web sites they
may link to. Any comments or suggestions can be sent by e-mail to comments@enslow.com or
to the address on the back cover.

Every effort has been made to locate all copyright holders of material used in this book. If any
errors or omissions have occurred, corrections will be made in future editions of this book.

Illustration Credits: AP/Wide World, pp. 3, 4, 9, 29L, 29R, 37, 40, 44, 47, 53, 56, 61, 63, 69,
72, 75, 79, 82, 86, 88, 98, 104, 107, 110, 113, 115, 116; Library of Congress, p. 18; National
Baseball Hall of Fame Library, Cooperstown, NY, pp. 14, 22; National Baseball Library, p. 91;
National Baseball Library (originally from *New York World-Telegram*), p. 35.

Cover Illustrations: AP/Wide World.

Contents

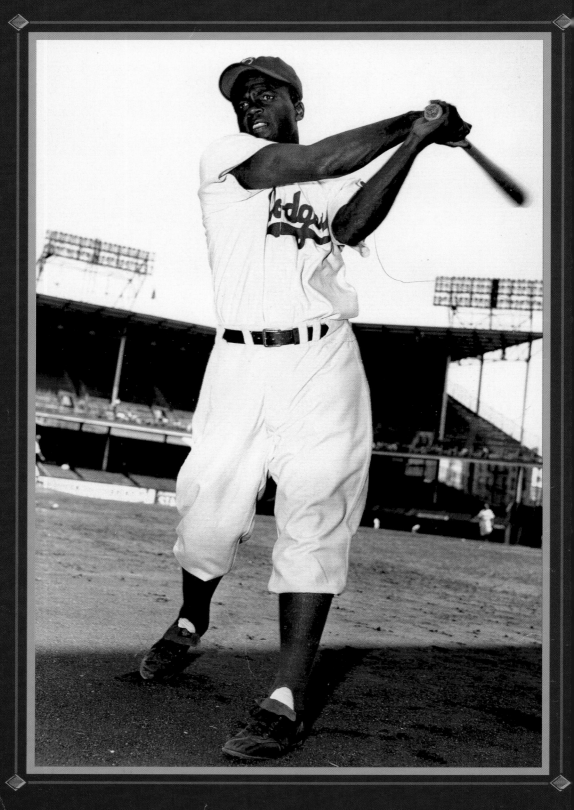

Chapter 1

The Experiment

Branch Rickey had a groundbreaking idea. The general manager of the Brooklyn Dodgers baseball team had been turning this thought around in his mind for a long time. He believed it was time to stop barring African-American athletes from major league baseball.

The year was 1945, and the major leagues were made up of white players—*only* white players. Rickey was determined to change that. "There is a Negro player coming to the Dodgers," he said. "I don't know who he is and I don't know where he is, and I don't know when he is coming. But he is coming. And he is coming soon."[1]

The most likely place to look for a talented black baseball player was in the Negro Leagues. Professional all-black teams had been competing since the 1880s. Occasionally they played against white teams, but mostly they traveled around the country playing exhibition games

> In 1945, only white men played baseball in the major leagues. Blacks played in the Negro Leagues.

against other black teams. This was called barnstorming. Starting in 1920, these teams were organized into leagues.

There were a number of outstanding ballplayers in the Negro Leagues, such as Satchel Paige, Josh Gibson, and Monte Irvin. Another excellent player—though not the best—was Jackie Robinson.

Robinson was twenty-six years old and playing for the Kansas City Monarchs when Branch Rickey decided to pursue his "experiment."[2] He needed just the right person. The player could not be too old. Satchel Paige, a standout pitcher, and Josh Gibson, an amazing power hitter, were both in their thirties. Monte Irvin was the same age as Robinson, but he was still in the U.S. Army. Other prospects, like nineteen-year-old Don Newcombe, were too young for the challenge. "No nineteen-year-old could survive the racist garbage," said Emil J. "Buzzie" Bavasi, a Dodgers executive.[3]

Robinson seemed like the best choice. He was the right age, he had a college education, he had played with white teammates before, and he was an outstanding competitor.

Rickey sent Clyde Sukeforth, a coach and scout for the Dodgers, to take a look at Robinson. Rickey wanted to know if Robinson had a good arm. He also wanted Sukeforth to find out about Robinson's habits, his speech, and how he handled himself. What kind of a person was

Robinson off the field as well as on it? If Robinson seemed right, Sukeforth had been instructed to bring him to Brooklyn, New York, to meet with Rickey.

Sukeforth did not know about Rickey's experiment. Instead, he had been told that Rickey was starting an all-black team called the Brooklyn Brown Dodgers. Rickey said the team would play in the new United States League. Their games would take place at Ebbets Field—the Dodgers' home—when the Dodgers were not in town.

Sukeforth traveled to Chicago and watched Robinson carefully. He liked what he saw. "The more we talked, the better I liked him," Sukeforth said. "There was something about that man that just gripped you. He was tough, he was intelligent, and he was proud."[4]

For his part, Robinson was puzzled. "Why is Mr. Rickey interested in my arm?" he asked Sukeforth. "Why does he want to see me?"[5] Sukeforth told Robinson about the Brown Dodgers.

The two men arrived at Rickey's Brooklyn office on August 28, 1945. Sukeforth introduced them, and Robinson sat down facing Rickey's mahogany desk. "Mr. Rickey went right to work on him," said Sukeforth. "He said, 'Jack, I've been looking for a great colored ballplayer for a great many years. I have some reason to believe you might be that man.'"[6]

Robinson waited for Rickey to ask him to leave the Negro Leagues and play for the Brown Dodgers. Instead,

Rickey said, "You were brought here, Jackie, to play for the Brooklyn organization."[7]

The Brooklyn Dodgers? Robinson was stunned. "I was thrilled, scared, and excited," Robinson said later. ". . . Most of all, I was speechless."[8]

Rickey asked Robinson if he thought he could do it. It was not an easy question to answer. First, there was some concern about Robinson's athletic ability. He had been a star in several sports in high school and college. As a ballplayer, Robinson was known for his amazing speed and his skill as a batter and as a fielder. But his ability had never been tested at the major league level. Was he good enough?

> "I was thrilled, scared, and excited. . . . Most of all, I was speechless."

Second—and perhaps the bigger issue—was the difficulty Robinson would face as the first black player to join the major leagues in the twentieth century. How would he handle the negative reactions he was sure to experience? There would be problems with his white teammates, with players in the other ball clubs, and with spectators in the stands. What would happen when Robinson traveled with the team on road trips? In the 1940s, many hotels, restaurants, and other public places—especially in the South—refused to serve African Americans.

Robinson had dealt with prejudice throughout his life. While he was not the kind of man to go looking for a fight, he did not back down when he came face-to-face with one.

Robinson and Branch Rickey, president of the Brooklyn Dodgers.

Yet Rickey made it clear that Robinson would not be able to fight back or respond to anything anyone said or did. Rickey did not want to give people the opportunity to say that a black player in the major leagues caused trouble. He did not want anything negative connected with Robinson's appearance on the Dodgers. "I need more than a great player," Rickey told him. "I need a man who will accept insults, take abuse, in a word, carry the flag for his race. I want a man who has the courage *not* to fight back."[9]

Rickey acted out the kinds of abuse Robinson would

have to put up with. He pretended to be a rude clerk who would not allow Robinson to spend the night at his hotel. He became a ranting baseball fan, shouting insults at Robinson because of the color of his skin. Then he was an angry teammate who did not want to play on the same team as an African American. He insulted Robinson's parents and his race and swung his fists in Robinson's face. "His acting was so convincing that I found myself chain-gripping my fingers behind my back," Robinson said.[10]

Separate . . . and Not Equal

The Civil War put an end to slavery, and in the years following the war, legal changes made African Americans full citizens as well as giving black men the right to vote. Then, in 1888, the first segregation law was passed in Louisiana, introducing the idea of "separate but equal." Even the white Americans who believed that blacks should have equal rights did not necessarily believe in social equality. The Supreme Court, in its 1896 *Plessy* v. *Ferguson* decision, upheld legalized segregation. Laws in the South—called Jim Crow laws—forced African Americans to sit in the backs of buses, use separate drinking fountains, and stay only at hotels for African Americans. Whites and blacks could not sit together in restaurants or movies, swim in the same pools, or send their children to the same schools.

Finally, Rickey challenged Robinson: "It's going to take an awful lot of courage. Have you got the guts to play the game no matter what happens?"

Robinson answered, "I think I can play the game, Mr. Rickey."[11]

> Robinson was about to face the biggest challenge of his life.

Three hours after he had first walked into Branch Rickey's office, Jackie Robinson signed an agreement with the Brooklyn Dodgers. He would receive a salary of $600 a month plus a $3,500 bonus. According to Rickey, Robinson would start out playing for the minor league Montreal Royals simply because he was not yet ready for the major leagues.

"I signed Robinson . . . because I knew of no reason why I shouldn't," Rickey said. "I want to win baseball games, and baseball is a game that is played by human beings."[12] He did not believe that skin color should be an issue in baseball.

Many people were in favor of Rickey's experiment. Yet even those who were ready to see black athletes in major league baseball were not certain that Jackie Robinson was the man for the job. They wondered if he was talented enough to play with the finest ball players in the country.

Perhaps most unsure of all was Robinson. But he was determined to prove himself. "I am some sort of guinea pig," he said. "But, hopefully, I'm going to be the best guinea pig that ever lived, both on the field and off."[13]

Chapter 2

Growing Up

J ack Roosevelt Robinson, grandson of a former slave, was born near Cairo, Georgia, on January 31, 1919. Jackie was the youngest of Mallie and Jerry Robinson's five children. At the time of Jackie's birth, his brother Edgar was ten, Frank was nine, Mack was five, and Willa Mae was almost three. Jackie was named for President Theodore Roosevelt, who had spoken out against racism—treating someone unfairly because of the color of his skin.

The Robinson family lived on a plantation owned by a white farmer, James Madison Sasser. In Mallie Robinson's mind, her husband's life working on the farm was not very different from the life of a slave. Jerry Robinson was paid only $12 a month, which was not enough for the family of seven.

Mallie Robinson talked her husband into asking Sasser to make him a sharecropper. This meant he would receive housing, land, and seed from Sasser and would be able to keep half of what he grew. Mallie worked alongside her husband, growing cotton, peanuts, corn, and potatoes as well as raising hogs, turkeys, and chickens.

But while Mallie Robinson was happier as their lives began to improve, Jerry was not. One day when Jackie was not even a year old, his father left home and disappeared from their lives forever.

Mallie Robinson was now on her own with five children to support and raise. Their future looked bleak in Georgia, so Mallie decided to move to California. In the late spring of 1920, Mallie and her children, her sister, and other family members boarded a train heading west.

In June, the family arrived in Pasadena, California, just outside Los Angeles. Mallie Robinson had exactly $3 to her name. She immediately began looking for a job and took a position as a maid with a white family in Pasadena. The Robinsons lived for a few weeks in a tiny three-room apartment near the train station. Then they found a house in a mostly white neighborhood in the northwest part of the city. By the time Jackie was three, the family had moved to nearby Pepper Street. Their roomy house had once been the town post office. The yard was filled with fruit trees such as apple, orange, fig, and peach. There was also a garden where they grew vegetables and flowers.

Although their living conditions had improved, the family had very little money. "Sometimes there were only two meals a day, and some days we wouldn't have eaten at all if it hadn't been for the leftovers my mother was able to bring home from her job," Jackie said. "There were other times when we subsisted on bread and sweet water."[1]

As some of the neighbors got to know the family, they helped out. For example, the man who ran a nearby bakery told Mallie to send her boys with a wagon to his store at closing time on Saturdays. His shop was not open on Sundays, so he gave the Robinsons any breads and cookies he had not been able to sell. The milkman would also

Mallie Robinson watches Jackie, left, as a young man, playing baseball with two boys outside the house on Pepper Street.

occasionally leave extra gallons of milk for the Robinsons.

> Food was often scarce in the Robinson household.

Mallie Robinson woke up before daylight to go to work and returned home tired. Yet whenever she was with the children, she gave them her full attention. Her greatest hope was that they would all be educated. Mallie Robinson impressed upon her family the importance of religion and treating others kindly.

For their part, the children took on a variety of odd jobs as soon as they were old enough to help. "We all worked after school to make a few dollars, cutting lawns, shining shoes, delivering groceries, running errands," said Mack Robinson.[2]

Even as a young boy, Jackie was aware of how hard his mother worked and that the burden of supporting the large family fell heavily on her shoulders. "At a very early age I began to want to relieve her in any small way I could," Jackie said. "I was happy whenever I had money to give her."[3] Jackie delivered newspapers and cut lawns for people.

Jackie's sister, Willa Mae, brought him to school with her each day because there was no one at home to watch him. Jackie played outside in the sandbox and Willa Mae kept an eye on him through the window. On rainy days, Jackie was allowed in the kindergarten classroom.

By 1924, Jackie had started school at Cleveland Elementary. He and Willa Mae often showed up at school feeling so hungry that they could barely stand. Their teachers, Bernie Gilbert and Beryl Haney, usually had sandwiches for them.

When the school day was over, Jackie had only one thing on his mind. "In those days he would come home from school, gulp down a glass of milk, put his books on that old dresser, and be out the door playing ball with the kids," said Willa Mae. "How that boy loved playing ball."[4]

Some blacks and Hispanics were moving to the area, and there were attempts to make sure the schools had a mix of students from different ethnic backgrounds. After two years at Cleveland Elementary, Jackie was transferred to Washington Elementary.

The first time Jackie had to deal with a racial incident was when he was about eight. A white girl in his neighborhood made fun of him for being black. Jackie's family had told him not to answer back when people made fun of the color of his skin. But Jackie was not one to back down from a fight. Soon he and the girl were involved in a shouting match. When the girl's father came outside, Jackie and the man began throwing stones at each other.

"We had a pretty good stone-throwing fight going," he said later.[5] The fight continued until the girl's mother put a stop to it.

The white people in Jackie's neighborhood did not want an African-American family on Pepper Street. They called the police with complaints, such as saying that

Edgar was too noisy when he skated on the sidewalks. They signed petitions to force the family to move. But Mallie Robinson would not be scared off. She "made it perfectly clear to us and to them that she was not at all afraid of them," Jackie said.[6]

In many ways, life in Pasadena was not too different from life in the southern states. Although local laws did not require segregation, business owners usually made sure the two races did not mix much. At the movies, African Americans sat in balconies that separated them from whites. The city swimming pool was open to blacks only on Tuesdays, and the YMCA would admit blacks only one night a week. At coffee shops, African Americans were hired to work in the kitchens, but they were not allowed in as customers.

Life was not easy for African Americans, and Jackie and his friends found ways to take out their frustrations. He and some other boys in the neighborhood formed the Pepper Street Gang. It was made up of nonwhite kids, including blacks as well as some Mexican and Japanese boys. The gang members stole small items such as "oranges, apples, and whatever else they could grab," said Rachel Robinson, who became Jackie's wife. "They would hang out in the rough of the golf course and steal balls off the course, wash them, and then take them to the clubhouse to sell."[7]

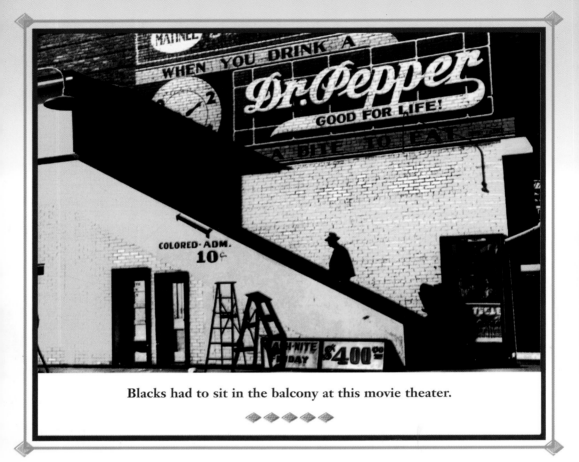

Blacks had to sit in the balcony at this movie theater.

The boys had several run-ins with the police. They were taken to jail at gunpoint one time for swimming in the reservoir. Other times, Jackie would encourage his friends to sit with him in the part of the movie theater reserved for white customers. Typically, the police would be called in to get the boys out of those seats. Jackie later said that he and his friends usually ended up at police headquarters at least once a week.

Two men came into Jackie's life who made a huge impression on him and helped turn him away from gang activities. Carl Anderson, who was a local African-American mechanic, kept an eye on what the Pepper Street Gang was doing. He pulled Jackie aside one day and told him he was not only hurting himself, but hurting his mother by his actions. Jackie later recalled, "He said it didn't take guts to follow the crowd, that courage and intelligence lay in being willing to be different. . . . What he said got to me."[10]

Anderson's comment made an impact on young Jackie. So did the advice of Reverend Karl Downs. Downs was a young minister who worked at the church Jackie's family attended, the Scotts Methodist Church. Jackie admired Downs's courage when he went against church officials and organized youth clubs to draw young people to the church.

A Mischievous Young Man

Jackie always enjoyed causing mischief as a young man. One time, when he was riding in a truck with friends, he spotted a heavy-set, well-dressed man on a street corner. Jackie lit a firecracker and tossed it at the man, close enough to scare him. Laughing, he also tossed one into the back of the truck where his friends were sitting. "*Boom*! Just like that!" said Jackie's old friend Jack Gordon. "He was more mischievous than anything."[8] Jack Gordon's wife, Rudi, described Jackie as "devilish."[9]

Downs was a good listener and Jackie trusted him. He often went to the minister with problems.

By the time Jackie was twelve and attending Washington Junior High School, it was clear that his main interest was sports. Combined with his natural athletic ability, Jackie had another quality that made him an outstanding competitor—he wanted to win more than anything else. It did not matter whether the sport was baseball, basketball, soccer, tennis, or marbles. Jackie always gave 100 percent.

> Two people helped turn Jackie away from the lure of the gang.

"I think it was 1933 when he was in junior high that we began to notice what an athlete Jack was," Mack Robinson said. "He just took up a sport and he was the best in the neighborhood before anybody knew it. I think the first time he played Ping-Pong he won the city championship."[11]

Jackie quickly became known throughout the area as an excellent athlete. Yet his older brother Mack was thought of as the true star of the family. Mack was a sprinter and broad jumper. He was on the U.S. Olympic team in 1936 and competed in Berlin, Germany. African-American runner Jesse Owens crossed the finish line first that year in the 200-meter dash. Mack came in second.

When he was sixteen, Jackie enrolled at John Muir Technical High School, known for its excellent athletics program. Although Jackie sang in the chorus, most of his after-school hours were spent playing sports. He played shortstop on the baseball team, competed in the broad jump and high jump on the track team, and also played key roles on the school's football and basketball teams. At this time, Jackie also began competing in tennis, a sport he had rarely played before. Still, with his excellent hand-eye coordination, amazing speed, and intense desire to win, Jackie took the championship in the Pacific Coast Negro Tennis Tournament when he was seventeen.

The football season of 1936 saw Jackie in the backfield on offense and also as quarterback. He became known early on for scoring touchdowns and helping the Muir Terriers win eighteen games in a row. In the last game of the season, Jackie's ribs were cracked when he was tackled. He could not finish the game, but recovered in time to take his spot on the basketball team.

The basketball team was not expected to do well that year. Several key players had graduated and the team was young. But Jackie was almost six feet tall and played forward. He was also captain and high scorer. The Muir basketball team wound up finishing in second place in the league.

Jackie had excelled at four sports at Muir High School, and several colleges were interested in recruiting him. But Jackie decided to start off at a two-year school.

> Jackie gave 100 percent to every sport he played.

Jackie, center, at home with his mother and brother Mack.

Chapter 3

College

ackie Robinson registered for classes at Pasadena Junior College in February 1937. Of the school's four thousand students, only about seventy were African American. One was his brother Mack, who was considered a top competitor in several track and field events.

Jackie played shortstop on the college baseball team that spring. He was an aggressive base runner and also hit well, so he was given the spot of leadoff batter. Robinson soon became known for his bold performance, something that would become his trademark throughout his career. During one game that season, he stole second and third bases—and then stole home.

Meanwhile, Jackie also became the school's second best broad jumper. His brother Mack set a national junior-college record, jumping twenty-five feet, five and a half inches. Jackie's best that year was twenty-three feet, nine and a half inches.

Jackie attended a summer baseball clinic run by John Thurman, the college's baseball coach. When fall arrived, Jackie was back on the football field as quarterback.

There were three black players on the football team. At first, several of the white players refused to attend practice. In fact, the conflict was so bad that the coach had to cancel practice. As Robinson walked away from the field, a friend called out to him, asking if they had finished early. "Naw, they don't want to play with us," Robinson said.[1] Eventually the coach was able to get the players working together. Robinson was a large force in making sure the team performed as a unit.

During the team's first scrimmage, Robinson chipped a bone in his right ankle and had to wear a cast for nearly a month. Without him, the team lost four straight games. When his ankle was better, Robinson came into the game as a substitute and scored a touchdown. All season, he dazzled the crowds with his brilliant rushing and passing.

Basketball season followed football, and Robinson had another excellent year. He missed being the highest scorer by one point.

Robinson's excellence was also obvious as he helped the baseball team capture the division title. His batting average was .417, and he scored 43 runs in 24 games.

Perhaps the high point of Robinson's junior-college experience was when he finally broke his brother Mack's broad jump record. Jackie jumped twenty-five feet, six inches. "I couldn't get over it, breaking Mack's record," he said. "Mack had always been my idol, making the Olympics and all that, and here I'd broken his record."[2]

Robinson's final football season at the junior college saw him help the team toward a record of eleven wins and no losses. Robinson scored seventeen touchdowns and 131 points. His honors including the Most Valuable Player award from the Pasadena Elks Club.

Perhaps more notable was Robinson's reaction when he was told on a team trip to Phoenix, Arizona, that black players would not be allowed to stay at the same hotel as whites. The coaches had not expected this, and persuaded the hotel management to give them rooms. Even so, Robinson led the other black players in refusing to check in to the rooms. To demonstrate their feelings, the handful of players spent the night sitting in the lobby.

A Liberal College

Pasadena Junior College was a very liberal college for its time. Black students could attend all classes. They could swim along with white students in the college's pool. They could take part in student dances. The only segregation was in the college's dance classes. Blacks could not go alone. They had to attend as part of a couple. This rule would help avoid having a black student dancing with a white student.

Robinson left junior college mid-year. He was one of the most sought-after athletes on the West Coast. Many colleges were interested in recruiting him, and he began taking classes at the University of California at Los Angeles (UCLA) in February 1939. A few months later, Robinson's life would change when tragedy struck.

Robinson had always been very close to his second-oldest brother. Frank had supported Jackie in every way. He scouted the players on other college football teams so he could advise Jackie on strategies. He also studied college sports programs, trying to decide which school would be best for Jackie. Frank was the one who had urged Jackie to transfer to UCLA.

On July 10, 1939, Frank was in a motorcycle accident. Jackie hurried to the hospital. There, he found Frank close to death and in horrible pain. Jackie ran home and buried his head in his pillows. Frank died the next day. After that, Jackie channeled even more energy into sports. It was his way of dealing with the pain of losing his brother.

Two months later, after playing in a softball game, Robinson was in a car with some friends. As another car tried to pass them, the driver—who was white—shouted out racial insults to Robinson and his friends. Both cars pulled over and fighting broke out.

When the police showed up, Robinson was carted off to jail. He was charged with blocking traffic and resisting arrest. He was released the next morning. Robinson pleaded guilty and was ordered to pay a fine. The sentence would likely have been harsher if Robinson had not been a popular local athlete. Officials from UCLA helped smooth things over and paid his fine.

Like most UCLA students at that time, Robinson commuted to school, rather than living on campus. Unlike most students, he was black. UCLA was a young school— its four-year program had been established in 1924. Determined to make a name for the school, UCLA officials encouraged talented black athletes to enroll.

Robinson's football career at UCLA began on September 29, 1939, in a game against Texas Christian University (TCU). The year before, TCU had been ranked number one in the nation. However, UCLA beat TCU by a score of 6–2, then won again the following week. Robinson was being called "the greatest ball-carrier in the nation" by many observers.[3]

Although Robinson missed two games that season after twisting his right knee, UCLA ended the season in a tie for first place in the Pacific Coast Conference.

Robinson had originally planned to limit his sports at UCLA to football and the broad jump in track and field. But basketball coach Wilbur Johns had seen Robinson play at Pasadena Junior College and knew he could use the athlete's help on his team. From the first game, Robinson was considered the best player on the team, scoring twenty-three of the team's twenty-eight points. Robinson went on to score a total of 148 points that season. While he excelled as an individual athlete, Robinson was always praised for his ability to put the team before himself.

He did not, however, play well on the baseball team that year. Although his fielding was strong, Robinson batted just .097 for the season. Robinson participated on the track team as well. At the Pacific Coast Conference championships in May, he broke the old conference record for the broad jump by jumping twenty-five feet. The next month, he won the National Collegiate Athletic Association title. No other student in the school's history had played four varsity sports in a single academic year.

Robinson did not play baseball during the summer of 1940. He played tennis and golf and worked in the property department of Warner Brothers film studio. When college resumed, Robinson was ready for another season of football.

It was at this time that Robinson met Rachel Annetta Isum. Rachel was a UCLA freshman who lived in Los Angeles with her parents. She had seen Jackie on the football field and thought he had too high an opinion of himself. Once she got to know him, Rachel changed her mind. "He was very impressive—a handsome, proud, and serious man with a warm smile and a pigeon-toed walk," Rachel said years later.[4]

Rachel Isum and Jackie Robinson had different goals. While his focus was on athletics, hers was on earning top

Jackie at football training at the University of California.
He was the best player on the UCLA basketball team, too.

grades in the university's nursing program. Still, they got along well and began dating.

UCLA had a poor football season that year. Robinson played well, however, and even set a national record for punt returns, averaging twenty-one yards. The basketball team did not do much better. But again, Robinson excelled and won the individual league scoring title. He had scored 133 points.

After two years at UCLA, by collegiate rules Robinson was no longer eligible to compete in football or basketball. He could have continued with baseball in the spring, but to the dismay of Rachel and his mother, Robinson decided he was done with college. He quit school in 1941, a few months before graduation. "I was convinced that no amount of education would help a black man get a job," Robinson said.[5]

Although university officials encouraged Robinson to remain in school and to graduate—they even offered him more financial support—Robinson wanted to begin working.

Chapter 4

Army Life

The world of professional sports offered few, if any, opportunities at that time to African Americans. So Robinson planned on a career in what he called "the next best thing"—a job as an athletic director.[1]

For the next several months, Robinson worked at a training camp for the National Youth Administration (NYA). The agency trained disadvantaged youths for jobs, which the agency would help locate. The NYA hired coaches, athletic counselors, and assistants. Robinson worked at a National Youth Administration camp located between Los Angeles and San Francisco on the campus of the California Polytechnic Institute in San Luis Obispo. The camp played other agency teams, and Robinson's first job as athletic director was to play shortstop on the baseball team. When he was not on the field, Robinson organized sports activities for the camp's residents, who were often poor and from broken homes. Robinson received a salary of $150 a month.

Robinson was busy with his baseball team as well as various exercise programs. Although most of the youths in the program were white, they did not seem to care that Robinson was a black man. The only time Robinson was reminded of this was when he tried to go to a dance at the agency and was not allowed to enter because of his skin color.

In August 1941, Robinson went to Chicago, Illinois, to play in an annual charity football game sponsored by the

> Robinson was becoming known as a fine all-around athlete.

Chicago *Tribune* newspaper. By then, Robinson was well known throughout the country, and many people thought he was one of the best all-around athletes ever. After practicing for three weeks, Robinson's team of all-star college players faced the Chicago Bears. The Bears, current champions of the National Football League, easily beat the college athletes, although Robinson was proud of catching a thirty-six-yard pass and scoring a touchdown.

In September, Robinson was given a chance to play football professionally, if only for one game. He played on the Los Angeles Bulldogs against the Hollywood Bears. Robinson injured his ankle in the second quarter and was unable to play the rest of the game. A week later, he was offered the opportunity to play semiprofessional football for the Honolulu Bears. In addition to receiving $100 per game, he would also have to work a construction job near Pearl Harbor, Hawaii, during the daytime hours. He decided to accept the position.

Robinson did not enjoy construction work. He was much happier on the football field. Advertised throughout the area as the "Sensational All-American Half-Back," Robinson drew people to the games.[2] He played extremely well until he once again injured his ankle. As attendance dropped, so did Robinson's interest in the league.

He headed home to California on the *Lurline* on December 5. It was only a couple of days into the voyage when the Japanese attacked the U.S. Naval Base at Pearl Harbor. The *Lurline* warily cruised the rest of the way home, with the crew fearing an attack by Japanese submarines. Robinson was still onboard the ship on December 8, when Congress declared war on Japan and, soon after, on Germany. The United States had entered World War II.

Before long, Robinson found a job as a truck driver for Lockheed Aircraft. The company had been reluctant to hire blacks in the past, but now that the United States was at war and there was a great demand for aircraft, more workers were needed. Robinson was back at home living with his family. He was also able to continue seeing Rachel, who was in her second year at UCLA.

Although Robinson registered to serve in the military, he was not especially eager to join the army. He wanted to

A Worldwide Struggle

World War II was a worldwide conflict that began in Europe in 1939. Although the war had its roots in Germany, it spread to include many countries around the world. Germany, Italy, and Japan were the major nations known as the Axis powers. They fought against the Allies, which included the United States, Great Britain, China, and the Soviet Union. The war ended in 1945 after more destruction and death than any other war in history.

help support his mother by working, and he was not sure his ankle could handle army training. However, Robinson was drafted on March 23, 1942. He reported to the National Guard Armory in Pasadena in April and was soon stationed at Fort Riley, Kansas, for thirteen weeks of U.S. army basic training.

African Americans were allowed to join the army in the early 1940s—but they were not treated as equals to white soldiers, and they were generally assigned to separate units. At first, the letters Robinson wrote home to Rachel were funny. He told her about being assigned to the cavalry, which meant he needed to ride a horse. However, Robinson had never felt comfortable on horseback, nor was he skilled at handling a rifle. He made fun of himself as he learned to become good at both.

Robinson in his army uniform.

While Robinson became an expert marksman and received high ratings for his character, his application for Officer Candidate School was ignored. Robinson knew he was qualified, and he was not given any explanation. Instead, he was told to take care of the horses at the fort. He was not even allowed to play on the army's baseball team.

While Robinson was in the army, Rachel also took part in the war effort. She was trained to do factory work for Lockheed Aircraft. During 1942, she worked the night shift in a Lockheed Aircraft factory. Then she changed out of her work clothes and into school clothes in the parking lot, and headed to UCLA for classes during the day. After graduating from UCLA, Rachel went on to the University of California School of Nursing. She carried a full load of classes as well as putting in eight hours a day in the hospital to become a registered nurse.

Robinson's time in the army was very difficult for him. He had dealt with prejudice throughout his life, but living in Kansas was quite another story. Kansas was less segregated than the Deep South, but even so, life was much harder for African Americans there. They were still treated as inferior to whites.

Around this time, Robinson met heavyweight boxer Joe Louis, who was also at Fort Riley. The well-known African-American boxer had important friends in Washington, D.C., and he used these connections to help

Robinson and several other blacks get fair consideration for Officer Candidate School that fall. On January 28, 1943, Robinson became a second lieutenant in the U.S. Army's cavalry. He became engaged to Rachel that spring.

Now that Robinson was an officer, he decided to join the baseball team at Fort Riley. "An officer told him he couldn't play," said Pete Reiser, who played on the Fort Riley team. "'You have to play for

Boxing champ Joe Louis.

◆ ◆ ◆ ◆ ◆

the colored team,' the officer said. That was a joke. There was no colored team. The lieutenant [Robinson] stood there for a while watching us work out. Then he turned and walked away."[3] Robinson did compete in table tennis, and he won the fort's championship.

Robinson was the morale officer in his army company. It was Robinson's difficult task to keep the spirits high in his all-black unit. The African-American soldiers at Fort Riley were unhappy about one of the rules at the post exchange on the army base. This was a store where soldiers could buy a variety of goods and services. The post exchange was usually crowded with long lines. Seating in the waiting room was segregated by race, and there were twice as many seats for white soldiers. The African-American soldiers ended up standing for long periods of time. Even if the white soldiers did not occupy all their seats, blacks were kept waiting until one of the six or seven seats designated for them was free. Robinson thought this was very unfair. "We were all in this war together and it seemed to me that everyone should have the same basic rights," he said.[4]

Robinson protested, and eventually he was able to secure more seats for the black soldiers, although whites and blacks were still required to stay in separate sections of the waiting area.

Robinson was asked to play on the army football team. Then, just before a game against the University of Missouri, Robinson was suddenly given two weeks' leave. He realized he had been sent home because Missouri would not compete against a team with a black player. When Robinson returned from leave, he told the coach that he would not play for a team that did not allow him to participate in all the games.

During this time, Robinson continued to have some problems with his right ankle. It had bothered him since

1937, when he injured it at junior college. An X-ray showed a number of bone chips, and Robinson was told to avoid doing army exercises such as marching and drilling.

In 1944, he had a serious disagreement with Rachel Isum. Both were strong-minded people, and they often butted heads on various issues. In this case, Rachel had written to him that she was thinking of joining the Nurse Cadet Corps in the armed forces. Robinson did not like the idea. He became jealous whenever he thought of Rachel being surrounded by so many servicemen. He told her not to become a cadet and threatened to end their relationship if she did join. Robinson was shocked when Rachel mailed back the bracelet and ring he had given her. The engagement was off, and Robinson promised himself that he would try to forget about Rachel.

When Robinson had completed his basic training, he was sent to a unit at Camp Hood, Texas, that was scheduled to go overseas. David J. Williams, a white second lieutenant in command of one of the black tank units, knew Robinson. "He was kind of aloof, very straight, dressed really sharp, didn't swear much," Williams said later. "He was a really good person, but he was never close to anyone.[5]

> "We were all in this war together and it seemed to me that everyone should have the same basic rights."

An unexpected incident suddenly changed the course of Robinson's military career. In fact, it almost brought it to an abrupt end. Robinson was riding a bus on the military base one day. At that time, Texas law required blacks to sit at the backs of buses while whites could sit in the front. But the army had ruled that there could be no separation of whites and blacks on military bases. Robinson took a seat in the middle of the bus next to a friend who appeared to be white, but was actually a light-skinned

On this public bus, all black passengers had to sit in the back.

African American. Robinson was soon ordered to the back of the bus by Milton N. Renegar, the white bus driver. "I refused to move because I recalled a letter from Washington which states that there is to be no segregation on army posts," Robinson said later.[6]

A heated argument took place. The bus driver threatened to make trouble if Robinson did not change his seat. Robinson would not back down. "I told him hotly that I couldn't care less about his causing me trouble," Robinson said. "I'd been in trouble all my life, but I knew what my rights were."[7]

When the bus came to a stop, members of the military police were called in to take part in the dispute. Robinson was placed under arrest and faced a court martial hearing. The trial was held August 2. Partially because of Robinson's reputation as a celebrated athlete and partially because some of the African-American officers wrote letters to newspapers telling about the court martial, Robinson was found not guilty of the charges.

While Robinson faced trial, his unit had gone overseas—landing at Omaha Beach in Normandy, France. He remained in the army for several more months. In November, he was honorably discharged. Robinson's three years in the armed forces were over. Once again, he was in need of a job, and once again, he turned to sports.

Chapter 5

The Negro Leagues

Robinson left the army on November 28, 1944. He needed a job and worried about this while he was waiting for his discharge papers. One day, he was playing catch with a black soldier who used to play for the Kansas City Monarchs, a team in the Negro Leagues. The two men began talking. The soldier's name was Ted Alexander, and he told Robinson that he might be able to earn a decent living playing in the Negro Leagues. Because of the war, teams were looking for players.

Although the level of play was extremely competitive, baseball in the Negro Leagues was vastly different from major league ball. Instead of taking place in stadiums, games were often held on sandlots and open fields on farms. The Negro Leagues baseball season began in February, running through the summer and well into the autumn. The teams generally played exhibition games throughout the South, where restaurants and hotels would not open their doors to African Americans. Rather than staying in hotels, players often slept on the team buses that took them from town to town.

"We hated the conditions, we hated not getting sixty cents on which to eat," said Walter "Buck" Leonard, who played for the Homestead Grays in the late 1930s and 1940s. "But we loved to play. We wanted to play. Baseball was our game."[1]

"We didn't get a chance sometimes to take a bath for three or four days because they wouldn't let us," said Ted Radcliffe, who starred in the Negro Leagues as a pitcher and catcher during the 1930s and 1940s. ". . . Most of the time we'd go into town . . . and we'd have to sleep on the floor of the railroad station."[2]

The type of ball played in the Negro Leagues was also different from major league baseball. It was a looser, faster-paced game where speed was more heavily emphasized. Runners teased pitchers by dancing off the bag and constantly threatening to steal the next base. Inside-the-park home runs were not uncommon and runners often advanced their way from first to third on bunts.

The Kansas City Monarchs was one of the more glamorous teams in the Negro Leagues. Better organized than most of the other teams, the Monarchs traveled with a generator and floodlights so that they would be able to play night games. The team drew large crowds and did

**One of the top Negro League teams was
the St. Paul Gophers, shown here in 1909.**

well financially. The players were treated like celebrities by the fans.

"You'd walk right by the stands and everybody knew your name . . . ," said Sammie Haynes of the Monarchs, "and the fans looked at the guys in our league as heroes."[3]

According to John "Buck" O'Neil, the Monarchs were similar in their popularity to the New York Yankees in the major leagues. The Monarchs, he said, were the "very tops. We had the stars and . . . we showed it to the world."[4]

Hoping to land a spot on the team, Robinson wrote a letter to Thomas Y. Baird, the owner of the Monarchs. Baird was interested, and the men quickly struck a deal—if Robinson made the team he would be paid $400 a month. Robinson showed up for spring training with the Monarchs in Houston, Texas, in April 1945. He had spent the previous few months at Samuel Huston College in Texas, teaching physical education. He was now ready to begin his baseball career.

Robinson was unsure of his skills because he had not played baseball for five years and considered it his weakest sport. But he led the Monarchs in hitting that season with a .345 average. He played in forty-five league games, hitting five home runs, four triples, and ten doubles.

Still, according to Robinson, it was "a pretty miserable way to make a buck."[5] He disliked the constant travel and hectic schedule, which had the players competing in up to four games a day. While his teammates did not visibly react to the unfair treatment of African Americans, Robinson grew angry when the Monarchs were turned away from restaurants and hotels.

Buck O'Neil, a Negro Leagues player who later became the first African-American coach in the major leagues, remembered the day the Monarchs pulled up to a gas station in Oklahoma. The team had been going to the same station for twenty years. Although they were allowed to buy gas for the team bus, the players had never been allowed to use the restroom. The sign hanging on the door said WHITE MEN ONLY.

"Jackie gets off the bus and starts walking toward the restroom," O'Neil recalled. "The man said, 'Boy, where are you going?' He said, 'I'm going to the restroom.' He said, 'Boy, you know you can't go to that restroom.' Jackie said, 'Take the hose out of the tank.'"

The owner of the gas station was surprised. He certainly did not want to lose a paying customer. But Robinson made it clear they would not buy gas unless the players could use the restroom. Finally, the man agreed to Robinson's terms. "From that day on, the Monarchs never got gas at a station [where] we couldn't go to the restroom" said O'Neil. "Jackie changed our thinking. He said, 'This is America, man.'"[6]

While Robinson was with the Monarchs, he was invited to try out—along with two other African-American players—for the Boston Red Sox. A movement was under way to allow blacks to play in the major leagues. The tryout was a step in that direction. Robinson did extremely well, hitting dozens of balls over the fence. Although the Red Sox were impressed with Robinson, he never heard from them after the tryout. As it turned out, the Red Sox would be the last major league team to allow black players in their organization.

After playing for the Monarchs for a year, Robinson was looking forward to quitting the Negro Leagues. He

Robinson got his start in the Negro Leagues,
on the Kansas City Monarchs.

> "Jackie changed our thinking. He said, 'This is America, man.'"

hoped to find a job as a high school coach and to marry Rachel. The two had been unable to forget about—or stay angry with—each other. Rachel had recently graduated from college.

Then, in August 1945 at Comiskey Park in Chicago, Brooklyn Dodger coach and scout Clyde Sukeforth approached Robinson. After the men talked, Sukeforth took Robinson to Brooklyn to meet Branch Rickey, the Dodgers' general manager. Robinson had no idea that the meeting would change his life as well as the future of baseball in America.

Wesley Branch Rickey's interest in putting an end to segregation in baseball had started more than thirty years earlier, when he was the student coach of the baseball team at Ohio Wesleyan University in Delaware, Ohio. That year, there was one black ball player on the college's team, a first baseman named Charles Thomas.

Rickey had traveled with the Ohio Wesleyan team to South Bend, Indiana, for a game at the University of Notre Dame. When the team arrived at the hotel, the clerk said no African Americans were allowed to stay there. Rickey alternated between yelling and pleading. Finally, the hotel manager said Thomas could sleep in the hotel as long as he stayed in Rickey's room.

When Rickey and Thomas went into their room, Thomas sat down and cried. Rickey said, "His shoulders heaved, and he rubbed one great hand over the other with all the power of his body, muttering, 'Black skin . . . black skin. If I could only make it white.' He was trying literally to claw the black skin off his bones."[7]

That memory stayed with Rickey. Years later, when he signed Robinson to a contract, Rickey said it was his way of trying to right the wrong that Thomas had suffered in 1904.[8]

Rickey told Robinson not to tell anyone about signing the contract—only Rachel and his mother. Rickey did not want to make the signing public yet. He was planning to sign a few other black players and then would release all the information at once. He also thought about waiting until the football season was over so people would pay more attention to the story.

By the fall, Rickey was worried the news would leak. On October 23, 1945, the Montreal Royals announced their decision to sign Robinson. In a room filled with newspaper and radio reporters, Royals president Hector Racine introduced Robinson as a new player on the Royals, a minor league team in the International League. The reporters were shocked for a moment and sat silently. Then they ran to their telephones to give the news to the radio stations and newspapers.

According to Racine, Robinson was being given a contract not only

> Branch Rickey knew he could not keep his big secret any longer.

First Major Leaguers

Many people think Jackie Robinson was the first African-American player to be on a major league team. There were actually a few African Americans who played major league ball in the late 1800s, but they were banned from the league not long after.

because of his excellent athletic ability, but because "we think it a point of fairness."[9]

Elmer Ferguson of the *Montreal Herald* rejoiced at the news. "Those who were good enough to fight and die by the side of whites are plenty good to play by the side of whites," he wrote.[10]

J. B. Martin, president of the Negro American Baseball League, congratulated Rickey on his actions: "I feel that I speak the sentiments of fifteen million Negroes in America who are with you one hundred percent and will always remember the day and date of this great event."[11]

However, not everyone was optimistic. Rogers Hornsby, who spent most of his baseball career playing for the St. Louis Cardinals, said, "A mixed baseball team differs from other sports because ball players on the road live much closer together. It won't work out."[12]

It would be up to Rickey and Robinson to make sure it did.

Chapter 6

The Montreal Royals

Not long after the momentous signing, Robinson went on a barnstorming tour to Venezuela. He traveled with other stars of the Negro Leagues. Gene Benson, a player with the Philadelphia Stars, said that Robinson did not spend much time with the other athletes. He enjoyed playing cards, but did not smoke or drink. To Benson, Robinson seemed like a man who was carrying a heavy weight on his shoulders. "He used to ask me all the time, 'Why did they pick me? Why did they pick me?'" said Benson. "He asked me that every other day."[1]

Rachel Isum and Jackie Robinson were married on February 10, 1946, in a lavish wedding. Rachel's mother had dreamed of a large wedding for Rachel, her only daughter. Rachel's gown was ivory satin, and the ceremony was held in a church in West Los Angeles. There were flowers everywhere and beautiful music. Robinson was happy and proud on his wedding day.

Jack Gordon and some of Robinson's other old friends played a prank on the newlyweds. They hid the car that the couple planned to drive away in after the wedding. The missing car did not reappear until most of the guests had left. "But even this final bit of deviltry couldn't spoil a perfect day," said Rachel.[2]

The couple took a honeymoon along the California coast, visiting San Jose and Oakland. Then they headed south for spring training in Daytona Beach, Florida. On the plane to Florida they carried a shoebox filled with Mallie Robinson's fried chicken. She knew what her son and his wife might have in store for them.

They did not have to wait long to find out. In New Orleans, they were removed from the airplane without explanation. Robinson argued, but he did not get anywhere. He and Rachel spent the night in a seedy hotel. For dinner, they sat on the bed and ate Mallie's fried chicken. "As we quietly ate," Rachel said, "I could feel humiliation and a sense of powerlessness."[3]

The Robinsons were able to fly the next day to Pensacola, Florida, where they were again bumped from the plane. They went to the bus station. Since there were empty seats at the front of their bus, they sat down. As white passengers came onto the bus, the driver ordered the couple to move to the back. Robinson did not protest because he did not want to upset Rachel. Later, when she was not around, he exploded in frustration.

Once in Daytona Beach, the couple stayed at a private home arranged for them by Rickey. They were not allowed to stay with the rest of the team in the hotel.

Robinson was welcomed to spring training at the ballpark in Daytona Beach. But in Jacksonville and Deland,

Robinson catches a ball in the infield on his
first day at practice with the Montreal Royals.

the team was locked out because of Robinson. In Sanford, they were "run out of the ballpark," said Rachel.[4]

The situation was extremely difficult for Robinson. It was hard enough worrying about making the team. Because of his promise to Rickey, there was not a thing he could do to respond to the racism he encountered.

"They say certain people are bigger than life, but Jackie Robinson is the only man I've known who truly was," said Hank Aaron, a Hall of Fame ballplayer. "To this day, I don't know how he withstood the things he did without lashing back. I've been through a lot in my time, and I consider myself to be a patient man, but I know I couldn't have done what Jackie did. I don't think anybody else could have done it."[5]

Putting up with the insults and abuse took its toll on Robinson. For a while, he went into a slump and was not hitting well. He found it hard to concentrate and even harder to sleep. He did not spend time off the ballfield with the white players. The black fans made him feel embarrassed and angry because no matter what he did, they cheered. By the end of spring training, though, Robinson's hitting returned along with his confidence. He won a permanent spot on the Royals.

> "They say certain people are bigger than life, but Jackie Robinson is the only man I've known who truly was."

The opening game for Montreal

took place on April 18, 1946, at Roosevelt Stadium in Jersey City, New Jersey. More than twenty-five thousand fans came to see Robinson's debut in the International League.

The Royals were playing the Giants, a minor league team of the New York Giants. When Robinson nervously came to the plate

The Montreal Royals

Montreal, Canada, was the first city in North America to have an African-American athlete on one of its top sports teams. The Montreal Royals were the AAA farm club—or the minor league team—of the Brooklyn Dodgers. Jackie Robinson played with the Royals for one year, during the 1946 season.

for the first time, he grounded out to the shortstop. In his second trip to the plate, he appeared a little calmer. With two men on base, Robinson smashed a fastball deep into left field. The ball went over the fence—more than 340 feet—for a three-run home run.

In the fifth inning, Robinson came to the plate again. He bunted and beat the throw as he raced toward first base. He then stole second base and moved to third on a groundout. It looked as if he were going to steal home. Robinson's movements down the baseline rattled Giants pitcher Phil Otis. Otis threw twice to third—and Robinson made it safely back to base both times. When it looked as if Robinson might steal again, Otis became so confused that he stopped his pitch mid-motion. This is

Montreal outfielder George Shuba congratulates
Robinson for hitting a home run in this game
against the Jersey City Giants on April 18, 1946.

called a balk and allows the runner to advance. The umpire waved Robinson home to score.

Robinson came up to bat two more times. By the end of the day, he had gotten hits on four out of five trips to the plate, stolen second base twice, scored four runs, and batted in three runs. The Royals came away with a 14–1 victory over the Giants. As Robinson made his way to the clubhouse, hundreds of fans crowded around him. This debut in the season opener seemed to erase his anger and worry of spring training.

There were other joyous moments during the season—but there were also difficult ones. When the Royals played a series against the Orioles minor league team in Baltimore, white fans screamed racial insults at Robinson. With many African-American fans attending the game, Robinson felt an obligation to play his best. He knew how much his presence on the field meant to them.

During one game of the series, Robinson did not play because of an injured leg. When the Royals won, the Orioles fans became furious. Perhaps because he was the most obvious target, Robinson became the object of their anger, even though he had been sitting in the clubhouse when the game ended.

Many of the Baltimore fans gathered together, waiting angrily for the players from Montreal to exit the field. There were no security guards. Most of the Royals had left, including manager Clay Hopper. Fortunately, several

Montreal players, including outfielder Johnny Jorgensen, waited with Robinson.

Jorgensen later said that the Baltimore crowd outside the clubhouse was yelling, "Come out of there, Robinson. . . . We'll getcha! We'll getcha!"[6] Hours passed before they finally moved on and the players were able to leave the clubhouse.

In Syracuse, New York, a player from the opposing team threw a black cat onto the field while Jackie was at the plate. He shouted out that the cat looked like Robinson's cousin. As always, according to the agreement with Rickey, Robinson could not express his hurt or anger in any way. He simply had to take it. That day in Syracuse, after the cat was tossed at him, Robinson hit a double and eventually scored. "I guess my cousin's pretty happy now," he yelled toward the dugout as he rounded the bases. This was as much of a comeback as he was allowed to give.[7]

When the team was not on the road, Jackie and Rachel Robinson enjoyed living in Montreal, Canada. They did not experience the racism there that plagued them in the United States. They rented an apartment in a French-speaking section of Montreal, and other than the language barrier, they got along well with their neighbors.

Rachel was expecting a baby, yet she managed to travel occasionally with Robinson when the team went on the road. At home, she helped Robinson through the difficult times by being constantly supportive. "She was his rock of Gibraltar," said Joe Black, who played on the Dodgers in the 1950s. "He said to Rachel, 'I don't know about this. . . . I wonder if it's worthwhile.' She just held him and said, 'You know, Jack, we knew it wasn't going to be easy.'"[8]

The anger Robinson had to keep to himself seemed to come out in part on the playing field. His batting percentage soared; he was leading the league in hitting by early June, with a .356 batting average. But the stress he faced took its toll, just as it had in spring training. Robinson often had trouble sleeping and many times could not eat.

> "You know, Jack, we knew it wasn't going to be easy."

Eventually, Robinson consulted a doctor, who told him he needed a rest away from the ballpark. He was not to read the newspapers or listen to the games on the radio. Rachel persuaded him to go on a picnic with her. That was all the rest Robinson could handle. He knew the team needed him and so he resumed playing after missing only three games.

Robinson's impact on the team was huge. By the end of the season, the Royals had won the division pennant.

Attendance had also been higher because of Robinson. Never before had a Royal won the league batting title. But Robinson did, hitting .349. Although he hit only three home runs, Robinson scored the most runs in the league with 113. He stole 40 bases and drove in 66 runs. He also had the league's highest fielding percentage at second base.

Robinson led the Royals to victory in the playoffs. The team played in the Little World Series against the Colonels of Louisville, Kentucky. Louisville fans had never seen African Americans in major league baseball, and they were nasty to Robinson. He played poorly in the first three games and the Louisville crowd screamed insults. Robinson recalled it as a "torrent of mass hatred . . . with virtually every move I made."[9]

The Royals were down one game to two as the series headed North to Montreal. Pulling himself out of his slump, Robinson helped the Royals overcome a 4–0 deficit to win the fourth game in extra innings and tie the series. The game went ten innings with the Royals coming out on top, 6–5. Robinson hit a double and a triple for a 2–0 win in the fifth game and the Royals won the series with a 2–0 win in the sixth game. Robinson's batting average for the six games was .400.

Montreal fans swarmed around Robinson, and he was carried off the field on their shoulders. The players and fans knew that Robinson's success story went far beyond the ball field. "You're a great ballplayer and a fine gentle-man," Clay Hopper, the Royals Manager, said after the game, shaking Robinson's hand.[10]

In California for the off-season, Robinson was next to Rachel when she gave birth to their son on November 18. He was named Jackie Roosevelt Robinson Jr.

Jackie and Rachel with Jackie Jr. at home.

For extra money, Robinson spent some time playing professional basketball in the National Basketball League. Although the Basketball Association of America did not allow black athletes, Robinson was offered $50 a game to play with the Los Angeles Red Devils.

At the end of his season with the Red Devils, Robinson wondered the same thing most sports writers and baseball fans across the country were wondering: When would he join the Dodgers?

Chapter 7

Welcome to Brooklyn

obinson left for spring training with the Dodger organization on February 20, 1947. Spring training had been moved from Florida to Havana, Cuba, that year. Rickey's idea was not only to keep Robinson away from the discrimination of the South, but to allow his new player to keep a low profile. He wanted to avoid any incident involving Robinson that could reflect badly on his decision to include black athletes in major league baseball.

By this time, catcher Roy Campanella and pitcher Don Newcombe were also in the Dodger organization with the Montreal Royals. Both men were African American. While all the other members of the Royals stayed at a cadet barracks at the Havana Military Academy, Robinson, Campanella, and Newcombe were housed in a

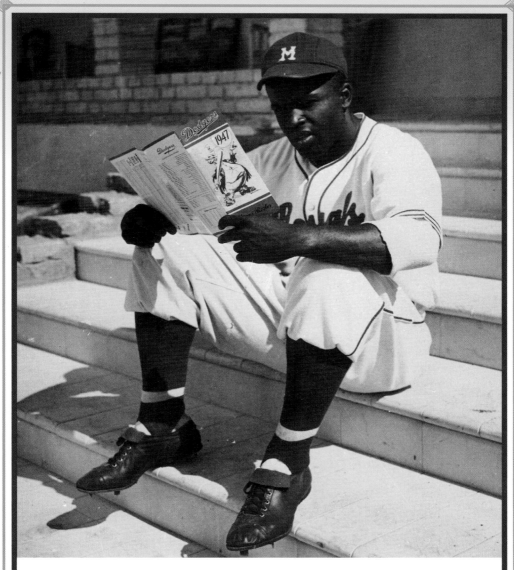

While he was at spring training in Cuba, Robinson looked over a list of the players on the Brooklyn Dodgers.

cheap hotel fifteen miles away from where the Royals held practice.

Robinson did not understand why the three African Americans were being segregated from their team in a country where segregation was not required by law. The separate housing was Rickey's idea. He worried that the black and white players might fight if they stayed in the same building. "I don't like it," said Robinson. "I don't like it at all. But I'll go along with Mr. Rickey's judgment. He's been right so far."[1]

Rickey was right to worry about problems among the players. As the Royals and Dodgers traveled around the Panama Canal Zone, Clyde Sukeforth learned of a petition signed by some of the Dodgers. These players said they would not play on the same team as Robinson. Sukeforth told Leo Durocher, the team's manager, about the petition.

The petition had come about partly because Robinson was playing so well. Rickey had hoped Robinson's skill as a ballplayer would encourage the Dodgers to welcome him onto their squad. After all, the more talented the Dodgers players, the better their chance of making it into the World Series. Robinson certainly showed his skill as an athlete. In seven exhibition games during spring training between the Royals and the Brooklyn Dodgers, Robinson batted .625 and stole seven bases.

Still, some white players did not seem interested in having Robinson join their team. They resented him, fearing they might lose their jobs to other African Americans. Many of the players—especially those from the South— had grown up with segregation and did not like the idea of having an African American on the team.

"The other boys—myself included—were not enamored about sitting at the table with Jackie," said catcher Bobby Bragan, from Alabama. "Dixie Walker actually put it in writing."[2] Right fielder Fred "Dixie" Walker was originally from Georgia and had moved to Alabama. Joining him in signing the petition were Bragan, relief pitcher Hugh Casey of Georgia, third baseman Harry "Cookie" Lavagetto of California, and two Pennsylvanians, center fielder Carl Furillo and second baseman Eddie Stanky.

Southerner Harold "Pee Wee" Reese had known segregation from the time he was a young boy in Louisville, Kentucky. Reese did not think it was right to keep Robinson off the team because of the color of his skin. "Skip me, Dixie," he said.[3]

When Durocher learned what was happening, he practically dragged the players out of their beds, calling a team meeting at one in the morning. "I hear some of you don't want to play with Robinson," he said. ". . . I'm the manager and I'm paid to win and I'd play an elephant if he could win for me and this fellow Robinson is no elephant.

. . . And here's something else. He's only the first boys, only the first!"[4]

Durocher told the players he did not want to hear another word about the petition, nor did he want to see it. Then he sent them back to bed. The petition was not mentioned again.

Robinson continued to play well that spring in spite of some illnesses and injuries. Before the ball club returned to the United States, Rickey spoke to the men: "No player on this club will have anything to say about who plays or does not play on it," said Rickey. "I will decide who is on it and Durocher will decide who, of those who are on it, does the playing."[5]

Back in the United States, Robinson met with Rickey in April, and the deal was made. He would be wearing a Brooklyn Dodgers uniform that season. Robinson would be the first African American to play major league baseball in modern times.

> "No player on this club will have anything to say about who plays or does not play on it."

He showed up at the Dodger clubhouse on April 11 and changed into his uniform—number 42. The team would play three games against the Yankees. Robinson would play first base.

It was a fairy-tale experience for Robinson. He was excited about playing at Ebbets Field as a Brooklyn Dodger earning $5,000 a year, which was then the minimum salary for a major leaguer.

Attendance soared above eighty thousand for the three games. Robinson played well, driving in five runs and committing no errors at first base.

Rachel and Jackie Jr. arrived in New York after the series ended. Robinson was thrilled to have his family back. They had been apart for two months and now cautiously took a room in a hotel as their temporary home. After all, as brilliant an athlete as Robinson was, who could say how long he would be playing for the Dodgers?

The Dodgers faced the Boston Braves on the season's opening day, April 15. According to *The New York Times*, Robinson's debut was "quite uneventful."[6] In front of a large crowd, Robinson did not play his best. He was unable to get a hit.

"I was nervous in the first play of my first game at Ebbets Field," he said, "but nothing has bothered me since."[7] He also said the reason he had not been able to get a hit was because he had difficulty with Boston pitcher Johnny Sain's curve balls.

Brooklyn "Bums"

The Brooklyn Dodgers have been known by many different names: the Bridegrooms, the Trolley Dodgers, the Superbas, Robins Daffiness Boys, Flock, and "Dem Bums." The team was located in Brooklyn from 1884 until 1957, when it moved to Los Angeles, California. The Brooklyn Dodgers also had the distinction of playing the longest major league game in history. It took place in 1920 and was a 26-inning tie with the Braves.

> "I was nervous in the first play of my first game at Ebbets Field, but nothing has bothered me since."

Sain recalled the day Robinson made his major league debut. "I don't remember our bench getting on him at all that day," he said. "We had a good ball club and thought we had a chance to win and didn't want to start the season with a fuss. Robinson was just another player to us. . . . He was a real fine gentleman."[8]

Robinson had his first major league hit the next day. Then the third game of the series was rained out. Still, the Dodgers had won the two games. By the end of the week—which included a series against the New York Giants—Robinson had gone 6 for 14, or 6 hits for 14 at-bats.

Since the start of the 1947 season, Burt Shotton had taken over as the new Dodgers manager. Shotton had been manager of the Philadelphia Phillies.

Attendance at Dodger games that season was huge. During their entire 1947 season, the team had its largest attendance ever, with 1,807,526 fans coming to the games. One radio announcer said Robinson was the biggest baseball attraction since Babe Ruth. The press flocked around him and Robinson was overwhelmed with invitations to dinners and parties. He received hundreds of letters, most of them praising his courage in breaking the color barrier.

**The Dodger's new first baseman played his first
major league game on April 11, 1947.**

Although many players in the Negro Leagues later said that Robinson was not the single best African-American athlete, they agreed he was the right person to integrate major league baseball.

Buck O'Neil believed Robinson was ideal for the job. "I know fellas at that time that were better than Jackie, but I don't think they would have taken the insults and things like that. He was the only one that could have carried that load."[9]

"He certainly had speed and all of that, but he had more than that," said Stanley Glenn, a catcher with the Philadelphia Stars from 1944 to 1950. "Jackie had the will to win. He had more heart than any man I've ever known. And he wasn't going to let anything defeat him. That was the big thing."[10]

It was not an easy load to carry. When the team went on the road, Robinson often felt lonely. Being the only African-American player in major league baseball made him famous—but it also set him apart from the other men. *New York Post* writer Jimmy Cannon called Robinson "the loneliest man I have ever seen in sports."[11]

According to one Dodger, "Having Jackie on the team is still a little strange, just like anything else that's new. We just don't know how to act with him. But he'll be accepted in time. You can be sure of that. . . . I'm for him, if he can win games. That's the only test I ask."[12]

Robinson was put to the test when the Dodgers played Philadelphia in late April 1947. He came as close to breaking the vow he had made to Rickey as he ever would.

The manager of the Phillies was Ben Chapman, who had been born in Alabama. Chapman urged his players to give Robinson a hard time. Throughout the game, the Phillies hurled racial insults at Robinson from the dugout. Robinson tried to ignore what was going on, but he could not. The words pouring out of the dugout were horrible and vicious. Robinson was fighting a huge battle inside himself. Part of him wanted to walk over to the dugout and punch the players; the other part knew he had to keep his promise to Rickey and not show his anger.

Distracted by the harassment, Robinson made his first major league error. But he also got a hit and scored a run and the Dodgers won all three games in the series. Unexpectedly, the Phillies' behavior angered some of the Dodgers, who spoke out in defense of Robinson. During the final game of the series, Ed Stanky—who only a couple of months earlier had signed the petition against Robinson—shouted at the Phillies, "Listen, you yellow-bellied cowards. Why don't you yell at somebody who can answer back?"[13]

If Chapman had hoped to turn all the players against Robinson, he was disappointed. His attack on Robinson actually brought the Brooklyn team closer together.

Robinson's first year as a Dodger had its ups and downs. He would get extra-base hits and then go hitless for many games in a row; he was applauded, then jeered.

Sometimes when Robinson was playing first base, runners would slide toward the bag, purposely keeping their spikes high in order to dig into him and draw blood. Pitchers threw at Robinson's head with the aim of hurting him, rather than just brushing him back from the plate.

There was also hate mail. Not only was Robinson attacked in the letters, but sometimes Rachel and Jackie Jr. were threatened, too. When the police were called in to

Robinson stole home in this game against the
Boston Braves at Ebbets Field on September 28, 1948.

investigate, the senders of the letters could not be traced, since they had given fake names and addresses.

Another serious reaction to Robinson's presence in major league baseball came right before the Dodgers were scheduled to play the St. Louis Cardinals. Some of the St. Louis players threatened to go on strike if they were forced to play against a black man. In addition to this, they said that the strike might go beyond the Cardinals and spread throughout the National League.

Reaction to the threatened strike was swift. Ford Frick, president of the National League, was known as a mild-mannered man. But he told the players they would all be suspended if the strike took place. He said he did not care if this destroyed the National League. The league would stand by Robinson and the decision to integrate baseball.

"This is the United States of America and one citizen has as much right to play as another," said Frick.[14] The strike never took place. The Dodgers won one game in the three-game series against St. Louis. The Dodgers and Cardinals were now tied for first place in the league.

The Dodgers traveled next to Philadelphia. Chapman, the Phillies' manager, was less hostile after being heavily criticized in the newspapers for his earlier behavior. But the city was not. The Dodgers were turned away from the Benjamin Franklin Hotel, where they had stayed in the past. The hotel manager told them not to return as long as they had a black athlete on the team. The Dodgers found another hotel.

Some of the Phillies ballplayers still showed open resentment of Robinson. They sat in the dugout, holding out their bats and making noises as if they were firing machine guns. Chapman, however, asked Robinson if the men could have their picture taken together. It was not easy for Robinson to agree, but he did. Harold Parrott, the Dodgers traveling secretary, offered to go along, but Robinson said it was something he had to do alone.

There were many things Robinson was forced to do alone. In Cincinnati, he could stay at the same hotel as the rest of the team, but was not allowed to use the dining room or swimming pool. In St. Louis, he had to stay by himself at the DeLuxe Hotel, which was only for African Americans.

Yet through it all—or perhaps because of it—the Dodgers were growing increasingly supportive of Robinson. In June 1947, Wendell Smith of the *Pittsburgh Courier* wrote that Robinson was "one of the boys."[15]

The teammate who received the most attention for his kind treatment of Robinson was shortstop Pee Wee Reese. During one game, when Robinson was being heckled, Reese walked over and put his hand on Robinson's shoulder. "People tell me that I helped Jackie," Reese said later. "But knowing my background and the progress I've made, I have to say he helped me as much as I helped him."[16] Reese valued Robinson not just as an athlete but as a human being. More important, he did not care about the color of Robinson's skin.

From April to June, the Dodgers' win-loss record had gone through leaps and dives, just like Robinson's season. Yet they would capture the National League pennant and finish the season with a .610 winning percentage.

Robinson seemed to hit his stride by mid-June. He racked up a 21-game hitting streak, missing the major league rookie record by one game. He also began to show off his dazzling speed by stealing home for the first time against the Pittsburgh Pirates. He was not elected to the All-Star team that year, but he received more than 300,000 votes, a good showing for a rookie.

Pee Wee Reese spoke up in defense of keeping Robinson on the Dodgers team.

The last day of the season, September 23, 1947, was celebrated as Jackie Robinson Day. Thousands of fans packed Ebbets Field to see Robinson receive such gifts as a television, a Cadillac, and silverware. Robinson's mother flew in from California for the event.

Robinson had had an excellent season, leading the Dodgers in runs with 125, hits with 175, extra-base hits with 48, runs batted in with 48, and a league-leading 29 stolen bases. In the 151 games he played that year, Robinson also tied with Walker in doubles (31) and with Reese in home runs (12). His final batting average was .297.

On September 30, the Dodgers found themselves facing

the New York Yankees in the World Series. It was the first time the Dodgers had appeared in a World Series since 1941. The Yankees won the first two games, and the Dodgers came back in the next two games to tie the series.

The Yankees won Game 5, but the following day, the Dodgers found themselves with a 4–0 lead in the third inning. Robinson had hit a ground-rule double to left field, allowing Pee Wee Reese to score. Then Robinson scored on a double by Dixie Walker. But the Yankees came back in the bottom of the inning to tie the game 4–4. Four runs by the Dodgers in the sixth inning eventually gave Brooklyn an 8–6 victory in Game 6.

The seventh and final game of the series was played at Yankee Stadium. Although the Dodgers took an early 2–0 lead, the Yankees came away with a 5–2 win and also claimed the title of World Champion.

Playing first base throughout the series, Robinson had hit a modest .259, scoring three runs, hitting two doubles, and stealing two bases.

He was voted the first-ever Rookie of the Year for his efforts on the field during his first major league season. Robinson also had his picture on the cover of *Time* magazine for everything he had accomplished *off* the field. It was impossible to call the 1947 season anything but a success for Robinson and the sport of baseball.

Chapter 8

Baseball
and Beyond

During the off-season, Robinson returned to California, where he played golf and relaxed. He also had an operation to remove a bone spur in his right ankle.

Now that Robinson was famous, various opportunities for making money came his way. He appeared in advertisements for bread, milk, and cigarettes. Robinson did not smoke. But at that time people were not aware of the dangers of cigarette smoking, so celebrities were willing to appear in cigarette ads. He had an offer to appear onstage, mainly answering questions about himself that had been prepared ahead of time. In the winter of 1947–1948, Robinson traveled throughout the South with this stage act. One unexpected result was that he gained a lot of weight. Few Southern restaurants at that time would serve African Americans, so Robinson dined in private homes.

His hosts made sure he was well fed, and his weight jumped from its normal 204 pounds up to 230 pounds.

Robinson worked hard to lose the excess weight. He wanted to be back in shape when he joined the Dodgers for spring training in 1948. That year it was held in the Dominican Republic. By then, another African-American player had joined the league. The previous summer, Rickey had signed the first black pitcher in the major leagues. Dan Bankhead had played for the Memphis Red Sox in the Negro American League. Bankhead and Robinson were still the only two black players on the Dodgers. But by the time the season was over, they would be joined by former Negro League catcher Roy Campanella, who had been playing for the Montreal Royals.

The Dodgers were back in New York in April 1948 to start the season. The Robinsons had moved to the top floor of a house in Brooklyn, giving them two bedrooms and a front porch. The neighborhood had mixed reactions to having a black family move into what was a mostly white area. A petition was circulated by some residents to prevent the family from moving into the house, but nothing came of it.

On their new street, the Robinsons made good friends with Arch and Sarah Satlow, who had three young children. Sarah helped answer Robinson's enormous amount of fan mail, so that it would be ready for his signature.

Jackie Robinson with rookie catcher
Roy Campanella in March 1948.

Rachel and Sarah would remain friends long after their husbands had died.

Robinson was still overweight at the start of the season. He vowed never to let himself get out of shape like that again. Throughout his life, Robinson tried to be a very disciplined person. He did not use alcohol or tobacco, he was a faithful husband, and he was a religious man, getting down on his knees each night to pray.

The 1948 season began slowly for him, and for the team, even though Robinson was now playing his favorite position, second base. Robinson eventually improved and wound up leading the team with a .296 batting average and batting in a team-high 85 runs. He also led the team in hits (170), doubles (38), triples (8), and runs scored (108). Yet Robinson was disappointed with his performance and believed he could have played better. The

Who's on First?

Robinson is best remembered as a second baseman, yet he began his major league career as a first baseman. That was his position when he won the Rookie of the Year award. When the Dodgers traded second baseman Eddie Stanky to the Braves in 1948, Robinson was put in his spot. He played there until 1953, when Junior Gilliam took the position. For the rest of his career, Robinson played left field and third base.

Dodgers had the poorest season they would have while Robinson played with them—they came in third in the National League.

Perhaps the most notable event of the season occurred in August 1948 when Robinson was tossed out of a ball-game at Forbes Field against the Pittsburgh Pirates. The umpire, Butch Henline, had made what many of the Dodgers considered a bad call while one of their players, Gene Hermanski, was at the plate. The Dodgers leaped off the bench in protest and began booing and shouting at the umpire. Henline warned the team to stop yelling. When Robinson ignored the warning, he was promptly thrown out of the game.

Even though he had been tossed out of the game, Robinson was happy: For once, the color of his skin had not been an issue. He was just another Dodger being disciplined for unruly behavior. "He didn't pick on me because I was black," said Robinson. "He was treating me exactly as he would any ballplayer."[1]

To make sure he did not gain weight as he had the year before, Robinson spent part of the off-season on a baseball tour with Campanella. The men traveled throughout the South and California. Robinson and Campanella then went to work for the Harlem YMCA in New York. For very little pay, the two men coached

"He didn't pick on me because I was black. He was treating me exactly as he would any ballplayer."

and counseled young people with great success—the Y's youth membership doubled. Robinson would volunteer time to the Harlem Y for the rest of his life.

During the fall, Robinson also began speaking on the radio. Six days a week, he did a fifteen-minute show on New York's WMCA. Robinson was a good speaker and enjoyed talking about a variety of topics—such as juvenile delinquency—along with sports.

Jackie went on the air talking about sports and other subjects, too.

By the time the 1949 season began, Robinson was earning $17,500 a year. For a player on the Dodgers, this was a good salary. Pee Wee Reese had earned $18,000 the previous year. The Dodgers were not a high-paying club compared to other teams in the National League. Cleveland Indians pitcher Bob Feller received the highest salary in baseball in 1948, bringing in $82,000 that year.

> Robinson enjoyed the time he spent coaching and counseling young people at the Harlem YMCA.

Robinson worked hard during spring training in 1949. After a slow start during the regular season, he quickly came into his own and was hitting .311 by the end of May. His average continued to climb—.344 in June and .361 by July 1.

Robinson's fine performance was recognized by the fans and helped put him on the All-Star team. Although the National League lost to the American League 11–7 in the All-Star game, Robinson still managed to hit a double and score three runs. The other two African American Dodgers—Newcombe and Campanella—were Robinson's teammates in the All-Star game.

In August, Robinson was still hitting around .360. He had developed a bruise in his left heel, but he continued playing. "They couldn't get me out of the lineup with a meat-axe," he said.[2]

To no one's surprise, Robinson won the batting title that year, hitting .342 for the season. He led the league in stolen bases (37) and finished in the top three in runs, hits, doubles, triples, and RBIs. That fall, he was voted the Most Valuable Player in the National League for 1949.

As for the Dodgers, they found themselves playing against the Yankees again in the World Series. The Yankees won the first game, 1–0. Game 2 was another close game. In the second inning, Robinson hit a double to left field, advanced to third on a short foul fly, and then scored on a single that was hit by Gil Hodges. This gave the Dodgers their only run of the game and they came away with a 1–0 victory.

The Dodgers and Yankees were tied at 1–1 through the eighth inning in Game 3. In spite of home runs hit by Pee Wee Reese, Roy Campanella, and Luis Olmo, the Yankees won 4–3. The Yankees also took Games 4 and 5 and once again, they took the world championship title. Robinson had hit just .188, with three hits and two runs.

During the off-season that year, he went on a baseball tour with Campanella and Newcombe. His team, the Jackie Robinson All-Stars, faced the Negro American League All-Stars. The games attracted large crowds.

Wilmer Harris, who pitched in the Negro Leagues in the 1940s and 1950s, also went on barnstorming tours, playing against Robinson as well as with him. "You can't imagine the crowds. It was magical," said Harris. "Jackie

Robinson drew many people that wanted to see him. Even housewives wanted to see him because he was a cult hero. All the parks were overflowing. In New Orleans, I remember particularly, they just let all the people come in from outside and they were standing behind second base. The outfield was covered from second base on with people. If you hit the ball over second base it was a home run. They didn't even care who won the ballgame. They just wanted to see Robinson."[3]

Back in New York, Robinson signed on to do two sports shows a week on TV as well as a daily show on the radio. He also launched a new career—starring in a movie.

Not long after the Robinsons had their second child, Sharon, in January 1950, shooting began in Hollywood on *The Jackie Robinson Story*. Robinson starred in the movie and played himself. He had taken young Jackie to Hollywood with him, while Rachel stayed home in New York with the new baby. But only two weeks after he left Rachel, Robinson missed his family. He also knew he would learn the script more quickly if Rachel were helping him. So Rachel traveled across the country with three-week-old Sharon.

"Jack and I rehearsed his lines at night, and early almost every morning," said Rachel.[4] A limousine came for them each day and they were driven to

> "They didn't even care who won the ballgame. They just wanted to see Robinson."

Robinson played himself in a movie
about his life, *The Jackie Robinson Story*.

the set where the movie was being filmed. Robinson found the move from athlete to actor fairly smooth. The director would explain how he wanted Robinson to behave, and Robinson was able to perform in front of the cameras as instructed. He was nervous, however, whenever he had to be physically close to his co-star Ruby Dee, who played Rachel.

When the movie opened in New York on May 16, 1950, most people praised Robinson's acting. The picture drew some crowds but did not make as much money as the movie studio had hoped. It followed the story of Robinson's life, centering on baseball, and it also dealt with the importance of democracy in the United States.

The 1950 baseball season began with the Dodgers favored to win the pennant. The race came down to the wire in September, with Brooklyn facing Philadelphia in the last—and deciding—game. Although the Phillies came away with the win, Robinson had had a good year. His batting average rose as high as .380 during the summer, but a slump in August brought him down to .328 for the season. He also hit 39 doubles, the highest of his career.

In 1950, Robinson had only twelve steals out of eighteen tries and his fielding was not as quick as it once was. Robinson was still an excellent ballplayer, but he was starting to show signs of slowing down.

Chapter 9

Number 42

The year 1951 saw some changes in the Dodger organization. The biggest was that Branch Rickey no longer worked for the Dodgers. A major financial disagreement had come between the man who had worked so hard to integrate baseball and Walter O'Malley, vice president of the Dodgers. When Rickey's contract expired at the end of October, it was not renewed. Robinson maintained a close relationship with Rickey for the rest of his life, but he wondered about the rumors he was hearing about being traded to the New York Giants. The trade did not happen, and Robinson remained on the Dodgers, earning $39,750 a year.

He spent that off-season as he usually did—working on radio and TV and helping out, along with Campanella, at the Harlem YMCA. During spring training, he once again battled with his weight and went on several diets.

The Dodgers were playing well as the 1951 season began. In May, Robinson again encountered prejudice.

The Dodgers had arrived in Cincinnati to play the Reds. Two men from the Federal Bureau of Investigation (FBI) found Robinson in his hotel room and told him that threatening letters, signed "Three Travelers," had been delivered to the *Cincinnati Enquirer* newspaper, the police, and the Cincinnati Reds. The letters said that someone across the street from Crosley Field would be waiting to shoot Robinson with a rifle.

The FBI warned Robinson not to go out on the field, but he was determined to play. Despite the threats, there was no trouble as the Dodgers won both games in the double-header, scoring a total of 24 runs. Robinson hit a home run in the first game.

The Dodgers were on a roll, and they made their way through the summer looking as if they would easily clinch the pennant. Then, suddenly, the New York Giants went on a streak. Although they had been thirteen games out of first place in early August, they closed in on the Dodgers so that it came down to a deciding game between the two teams on October 3. The Dodgers pulled ahead to lead 4–2, but in the ninth inning, a Giants home run gave New York the victory.

The season had been a good one for Robinson. He hit .338, batted in 88 runs, and hit 19 home runs. He also had the best fielding percentage—.992—in the league. At the time it was the highest ever earned by a second baseman.

During 1952 spring training, a rookie named Joe Black

Hate mail threatening Robinson's life did not
stop him from playing at Crosley Field in Cincinnati.

joined the Dodgers. He had played in the Negro Leagues. Robinson asked Black—a large man—how much he weighed. Black said 220 pounds. "You can fight too, can't you?" Robinson asked. Black said he could, and he later recalled that Robinson stated, "But we're not gonna fight." It had been five years since Robinson had broken the color barrier in major league baseball. So Black was surprised when Robinson said, "They're gonna call you names and they're gonna do something, you won't know what exactly, but it will be something—and we're not gonna fight."[1]

Although the team was playing well, Robinson had some personal distractions during the season. Rachel gave birth to their third child, David, in May. She developed a kidney infection and had to stay in the hospital. Soon after, she had to undergo an operation for what doctors feared might be a cancerous tumor in her breast.

The Dodgers were playing the St. Louis Cardinals in Missouri, and Robinson quickly left and flew home to be with his wife. He was immensely relieved when the doctors said Rachel did not have cancer after all. Yet the worry took its toll on him and it was not until the end of August that he brought his slumping average up to .300.

The Dodgers were able to secure first place, partly thanks to their new pitcher Joe Black. Once again, they would be facing the Yankees in the World Series—but Robinson would not be playing his best.

Although the Yankees were heavily favored, the Dodgers took the first game by a score of 4–2 at Ebbets Field. Nearly thirty-five thousand spectators watched as Robinson hit a home run in the second inning. Duke Snider followed with a home run in the sixth, and then Pee Wee Reese hit another in the eighth.

The Yankees evened the score in Game 2 but the Dodgers took the third game. The Yankees won Game 4, but the Dodgers were able to pull off an eleventh-inning victory in Game 5. The sixth game brought the series to a tie, setting the stage for a deciding Game 7.

The seventh game was played at Ebbets Field. The game was tied at 2–2 going into the sixth inning, but a home run by Mickey Mantle in the sixth and another New York run in the seventh put the Yankees ahead 4–2. A New York win was in jeopardy when the Dodgers loaded the bases in the seventh inning with two outs. Robinson came up and, on a 3–2 count, hit what looked like a routine pop-up. Yet none of the Yankees seemed to react to the fly ball as the Dodgers raced around the bases. Then suddenly, second baseman Billy Martin made an amazing catch, which put an end to the Dodgers' rally. Once again, New York took the title of "world champions."

Robinson was disappointed about the outcome of the series and his .174 average. But he was pleased that he had helped the Dodgers take the pennant that year. His thoughts about retirement were still on the back burner.

He wanted to continue making a difference in the country's treatment of African Americans. He knew baseball was his most obvious way of doing that.

Meanwhile, the Jackie Robinson Store opened in the late fall of 1952. It was a men's clothing store located in Harlem. Robinson made little money from the store during the six years he was involved in it. His money was also invested in real estate. He planned to build the Jackie Robinson Apartments on a lot he had bought in the Bronx. In addition, he was able to make money promoting such products as party favors and drinking glasses.

The 1953 season was a strong one for the Dodgers. Robinson, along with four other teammates, had batting averages above .300. Robinson hit .329, with 12 home runs and 95 RBIs.

For the fourth time in Robinson's major league career, he found himself in a World Series facing the Yankees. He also became the first player to start at three different positions in the World Series. He played first base in 1947, second base in 1949 and 1952, and left field in 1953.

The Dodgers ("Dem Bums" from Brooklyn) were ready for their challenge against the Yankees (the "Bronx Bombers"). Because both teams' stadiums could be reached on New York subway lines, the World Series was nicknamed the "Subway Series." In 1953, the Yankees were hoping to win their fifth title in a row, while the Dodgers desperately wanted to come out on top for once.

The Yankees won the first two games, but the Dodgers' fortunes would change in the third game. Robinson had so far gone one-for-eight in the series. In the fifth inning, he hit a double to right field and advanced to third base on a balk by the pitcher. He then scored the Dodgers' first run. In the sixth inning, with two outs, Robinson hit a single to left field, scoring Duke Snider. An eighth-inning home run by Roy Campanella sealed the Dodgers' 3–2 win. Snider's two doubles and a home run in the fourth game secured a 7–3 victory for the Dodgers.

But the Yankees came back to win Game 5 and Game 6. For the fifth year in a row, the Yankees were World Champions. Robinson had gotten eight hits—including two doubles—in the course of the six games and wound up with a .320 series batting average.

Robinson took his exhibition all-star team on the road again after the series had ended. Thousands of fans showed up to see the games. Robinson's team now had three white players on it—Gil Hodges, Ralph Branca, and Bobby Young. Officials in both Memphis, Tennessee, and Birmingham, Alabama, were strongly against having blacks and whites playing together. To avoid trouble, the white athletes did not play in those games. When Robinson was later asked why he agreed to segregated play, he said that at the time it had seemed the right thing to do based on advice he had received from both blacks and whites.

With spring training looming before him, Robinson became chairman of the Commission on Community Organization of the National Conference of Christians and Jews (NCCJ). He supported the NCCJ belief that if different groups discover what they have in common, they can come up with solutions for solving conflicts. He went on a tour across the country in February. He talked to thousands of people about the need for different races to get along and the importance of religion and education.

The 1954 season saw another change in the Dodgers management. Walter Alston was the new manager. Adjusting to Alston was difficult for Robinson. Later, Robinson would describe him as the worst manager he had ever played for. Robinson was also having trouble adjusting to his now thirty-five-year-old body. It was getting more difficult every year to lose the weight he was putting on during the off-season, and as a result his knees often bothered him.

Although he started out strong during the 1954 season—hitting .351 in June—Robinson struggled at times. Partly due to injuries, his 1954 season stolen bases (7) and runs batted in (59) were the fewest of his career. He did, however, bat .311, with 22 doubles and 15 home runs.

The Dodgers did not win the pennant that year, and Robinson was considering retirement. By this time, he had moved his family to a large house in Stamford, Connecticut. The Robinsons had built the home on six acres of land. It had an open design with a lot of glass and granite. The house was one of the many expenses Robinson was faced with, and he needed his Dodgers salary. Yet he was getting ready to leave baseball. Quite simply, he was tired. He had put up with a lot through the years, and he had had enough. He also knew that his body was not going to last much longer.

"Jack changed a little at the end," said Duke Snider. "He got a little sour. . . . He always felt the umpires gave him a hard time, and when he was called out on a close play he would scream at them from the bench. . . . Jackie could be stubborn about those things. He was such a great competitor, such a hard-nosed player."[2]

Robinson did not go on an off-season baseball tour in 1954. Instead, he played golf in Connecticut and went on a tour for the NCCJ. He also began working on a committee for the United Negro College Fund.

The Dodgers opened the 1955 season with a ten-game winning streak. But by May, Robinson was so unhappy with how he was playing that he asked Alston to take him out of the lineup. He was hitting below .250 and could not seem to improve. Alston wanted to keep him in the lineup if for no other reason than to motivate his teammates. He moved Robinson from left field to third base.

During the next month, Robinson batted .328. Yet halfway through the season, he was forced to miss games because of injuries, especially to his knees and ankles. For

**Happy birthday! Robinson's family
helped him celebrate turning thirty-five.**

six years, he had been voted to the All-Star team—but not
in 1955.

Although Robinson's baseball career was drawing to a
close, his impact on the sport was still being felt. Nearly
forty African-American athletes were playing major league
baseball and the only teams that had yet to integrate were
the Philadelphia Phillies, the Detroit Tigers, and the
Boston Red Sox.

By September 1955, Robinson went through a period

of playing well, and the Dodgers found themselves in yet another Subway Series with the Yankees.

Close to sixty-four thousand spectators packed into Yankee Stadium to watch the start of the World Series. Don Newcombe was on the mound for the Dodgers. Although he had been a twenty-game winner during the regular season—and although Robinson stole home in the eighth inning, lighting a fire under the Dodgers—Newcombe was not able to come away with a win in the first game. The Yankees won, 6–5. In the second game, the Dodgers were not able to do any better. Eight Yankee hits helped them on their way to a 4–2 victory.

But the tide turned in Game 3. Pitcher Johnny Podres, who had compiled only a 9–10 record for the Dodgers during the regular season, was facing Bob Turley, the Yankee's seventeen-game winner. With the score tied 2–2 in the bottom of the second inning, Robinson stepped up to the plate. He hit a single to center field and then scored when Junior Gilliam was walked with the bases loaded. The Dodgers now had a 3–2 lead and went on to win, 8–3.

The Dodgers won Game 4, and the series was tied at two games apiece. Game 5 saw Roger Craig, a rookie pitcher, on the mound for Brooklyn. Craig was the winning pitcher, putting the Dodgers ahead with a 5–3 victory.

Game 6 could have secured the World Championship title for the Dodgers. But Whitey Ford held Brooklyn to four hits and one run. The Yankees came away with the 5–1 victory.

Johnny Podres pitched again for the Dodgers in the deciding seventh game. Robinson was forced to sit out this game, complaining of pain in his right heel. Podres never allowed the Yankees to score. The Dodgers won 2–0, giving Brooklyn their first-ever World Series championship.

Although Robinson had not been able to play in the final game, he took away with him the distinction of having held four different positions in World Series games. He was also still heavily praised by sportswriters for his important role on the team.

But he was not sure if he had any baseball left in him as he headed to New York's Catskill Mountains during the off-season. He had hit only .256 in 1955 and driven in a mere 36 runs. His 81 hits were the lowest of his career, only half the number of hits he had achieved just two years earlier.

In the end, Robinson returned to baseball for one more year. In 1956 he helped the Dodgers win their sixth pennant since he had joined the team. Meanwhile, it seemed as if Robinson was not the only one who would soon be leaving Brooklyn. Ebbets Field was an old stadium—the first game had been played there in 1913. It was in poor shape and Dodgers officials were trying to figure out what to do. It was decided that over the next three years the team would play twenty of its home games at Roosevelt Stadium in Jersey City.

Robinson reportedly made negative remarks about having a major league team play in Jersey City in 1956. He was booed on the field and wound up hitting .275, with 43 RBIs and 98 hits—his second worst season in the major leagues. He stole home for the last time during regular season play on April 25 against the Giants. It was the nineteenth time he had done this in his career.

The Dodgers won the pennant and again were up against the Yankees in the World Series. This would be Robinson's sixth trip to the Series and he played in all seven games.

The Dodgers looked strong at Ebbets Field when, helped by Robinson's second-inning home run, they won the first game 6–3. In Game 2, the Dodgers again came out on top, triumphing over the Yankees 13–8. But the "Bronx Bombers" came back when the series moved to Yankee Stadium in the third game. Behind the pitching of Whitey Ford, the Yankees won 5–3. In Game 4, the Yankees again beat the Dodgers. Helped by home runs from Mickey Mantle and Hank Bauer, they won 6–2.

The series was now tied at two games each when the historic Game 5 was played. On the mound for the Yankees was Don Larsen, a twenty-seven-year-old right-hander. Although Robinson hit a sharp line drive, he was thrown out at first. In the top of the fifth, Gil Hodges hit a ball that seemed a certain home-run, but Mickey Mantle made an incredible catch with an outstretched glove. Sandy Amoros also hit a ball that seemed as if it would be a home run, but it went foul. Larsen went nine innings without allowing a runner on base. He had pitched the first—and as of this date the only—perfect game in a World Series. The Yankees won, 2–0.

Game 6 was scoreless after nine and half innings. Robinson came up to the plate in the bottom of the tenth. With two men on base, he hit a line drive into left field. Yankee outfielder Enos Slaughter was unable to field the ball and it became the game-winning single. The Dodgers won in ten innings, by a score of 1–0.

Brooklyn was not able to come back the following day. The team was held to only three hits in the seventh game and the Dodgers did not score a run. Helped by two home runs from Yogi Berra, the Yankees took Game 7 and the World Championship by a score of 9-0.

Although Robinson said after Game 6 that he was feeling "like a kid again," he was now thirty-seven years old and his hair was gray.[3] He went on a twenty-game tour of Japan with the Dodgers and when he returned to the United States, he spent much of his time speaking on behalf of the NCCJ.

Robinson had definitely decided to quit baseball, and the question of what he should do next was answered as 1956 drew to a close. His financial adviser, Martin Stone, had been looking for a business position for Robinson. Stone found it at the Chock Full o' Nuts coffee shop chain. Robinson was offered the position of director of personnel for the company. He signed a contract, although he had not yet told the Dodgers of his plans.

Robinson spoke with Dodgers officials right after signing the Chock Full o' Nuts contract. He was told he had been traded to the New York Giants. The Dodgers were to receive pitcher Dick Littlefield and $35,000 in exchange for Robinson. But there would be no trade. Robinson was retiring from baseball and turning to the world of business.

In January 1957, he cleaned out his locker at Ebbets Field. "So I'm through with baseball," Robinson said. "From now on, I'll be just another fan—a Brooklyn fan. I'm through with baseball because I know that, in a matter of time, baseball would have been through with me."[4]

Robinson said he had no regrets about leaving the game. "There are lots of things I'll miss. I love baseball and I'll miss playing the game. . . . There are a few things I'd like to forget, like the insults from other dugouts that first year, and all the times I blew my top when I shouldn't have. . . . But most of the irritations of those days I've forgotten. I've never taken my baseball home with me."[5]

The year after Robinson retired, the Brooklyn Dodgers left Ebbets Field as well and moved to their new home in Los Angeles.

After ten years with the Brooklyn Dodgers, Robinson,
age thirty-eight, said good-bye to his career in baseball.

Chapter 10

The Final Years

S oon after he retired from baseball, Robinson began a tour across the country for the National Association for the Advancement of Colored People (NAACP). Robinson had been given a $10,000 check from Chock Full o' Nuts as a donation to the NAACP's Fight for Freedom Fund. The goal of the fund was to raise a million dollars each year. The money would then be used for legal fees for lawsuits challenging segregation. Robinson was chairman of the 1957 fund drive.

Trips such as these took up a lot of Robinson's time. He traveled widely, speaking on behalf of the NAACP, the NCCJ, and a war veterans organization.

Although Robinson gladly gave of his time, he was now beginning to have some serious health problems. His body was showing severe signs of wear and tear. Robinson had developed diabetes, so he had to stop eating the ice cream, pies, and cakes that he enjoyed so much. He had to learn how to inject himself with insulin, which would help control how much sugar was in his blood.

Robinson had kept his diabetes a secret from his teammates and coaches. He had wanted to keep playing as long as possible. Baseball was not only his way of earning a living, but the best way for him to make a difference in the lives of all African Americans.

Now Robinson was busy with his job as head of personnel for Chock Full o' Nuts. He drove into New York City every day in a large blue Chrysler, making the drive to work a competitive challenge for himself. He mapped out a few different routes for getting to work and studied the traffic patterns. He timed every trip he made. He wanted the drive to work to take the shortest possible time, and he left nothing to chance.

Robinson enjoyed his work and kept only one item on his desk that showed he had been a sports star—a football shoe from his days at UCLA. As director of personnel, Robinson made note of the workers' wages, benefits, and chances for promotion. Most Chock Full o' Nuts workers were black, and he took a special interest in them. He traveled to the different coffee shops and talked to the employees, hoping to identify problems.

Robinson's civil rights work put him in contact with political leaders, such as Vice President Richard Nixon. The two men got along extremely well. Nixon had attended the football game in 1939 when UCLA played the University of Oregon, and Robinson was thrilled to discuss the game—in which he had been a key player—in detail. Robinson believed Nixon would help the cause of civil rights. In 1958, there was a rumor that Robinson himself might run for political office. But he quickly stated that he was not interested.

Robinson shared his baseball expertise
with Jackie Jr. and his Little League teammates.

In 1959, Robinson turned forty and began a once-a-week interview show on the radio. On the half-hour program, called the *Jackie Robinson Show*, he interviewed many political figures, including Eleanor Roosevelt, wife of former president Franklin Delano Roosevelt. Later that year, Robinson also began writing a newspaper column for the *New York Post*. His column, "Jackie Robinson," appeared in the sports section. Robinson wrote about sports-related topics as well as political issues, particularly civil rights.

The following year, he took a break from both his column and his job at Chock Full o' Nuts. He decided to spend all his time working on Nixon's presidential campaign. He believed Nixon was stronger than the other candidate—John F. Kennedy—on civil rights. He later regretted supporting Nixon. Traveling from New York to California, Robinson spoke on behalf of Nixon. When Nixon was defeated in the election, Robinson went back to work at Chock Full o' Nuts. He continued devoting his free time to the civil rights movement.

One of Robinson's accomplishments was helping to start a Student Emergency Fund in 1960. The purpose of the fund was to raise money that would help students in the South who were holding demonstrations to protest the unfair treatment of blacks.

There had been some changes in Robinson's home life over the past few years. Rachel had earned a master's degree in psychiatric nursing from New York University. She got a job as a clinical nurse in a hospital in the Bronx. Although she still made sure she got up every morning with the children and saw them off to school, she spent the greater part of the day away from home. Robinson had mixed feelings about the many hours his wife was working. He was pleased that she was happy, but he missed her.

Rachel's mother, Zelee, now lived with the Robinson family, and she helped with the children. This was not always an easy task. Jackie Jr. had trouble in school and in spite of great athletic talent, had very little interest in sports. When he entered his teens, Jackie Jr. was sent to the Stockbridge School in Massachusetts, where it was hoped that he would do better with more personal attention.

Early in 1962, Robinson learned he was going to be inducted into the National Baseball Hall of Fame in Cooperstown, New York. He wrote in a newspaper column: "If this can happen to a guy whose parents were virtually slaves . . . a guy whose mother worked . . . from sunup to sundown . . . then it can happen to you."[1]

The Hall of Fame induction took place on July 23, 1962. Crowds of people waited to hear Robinson's speech. A young boy got pushed down by the crowd and dropped his glove. Robinson helped the boy to his feet, handed him the glove, and smiled. The boy asked Robinson if he would autograph the glove, which Robinson gladly did.

Robinson, the first African American to be in
the National Baseball Hall of Fame, holds his plaque.

THE FINAL YEARS

In his speech, Robinson thanked the three people who had advised him throughout his life—Branch Rickey, Mallie Robinson, and Rachel. "I have been on 'Cloud Nine' since learning of the election," he said. ". . . and I don't think I'll ever come down."[2]

Robinson entered Mount Vernon Hospital for an operation on January 7, 1963. The problem was his knee, which had torn cartilage. Although he should have been discharged from the hospital after only a few days, he wound up staying there for weeks. His knee had become infected after the operation, and bacteria from the infection had spread throughout his body. His diabetes was also affected by this. For days, Robinson drifted in and out of consciousness. As he finally began to get better, he had numerous visitors, including Branch Rickey, who was eighty-one years old.

Robinson's homecoming, in bandages and on crutches, was not easy. When it was time for dinner on his first day back, the family discovered that Jackie Jr. was missing. He had been living at home in Connecticut again, attending the public high school, after being dismissed from the boarding school because of poor schoolwork and fighting.

The family learned Jackie Jr. had withdrawn all his money from the bank and run away. He and a friend had gone to California by bus. The boys had thought they could get jobs picking fruit, but it was too early in the season. Jackie Jr. called home, and two weeks later he was back with his parents.

Although Robinson could not get around easily anymore—he used a cane—he began to write a newspaper column once again. This time, it was for the *Amsterdam News*, a black weekly in New York. His column ran on the paper's editorial page and focused mainly on criticizing national efforts at civil rights.

Robinson also worked toward opening a bank in Harlem, an African-American neighborhood of New York City. African Americans had long been discriminated against at banks. It was hard for them to get mortgages to buy homes or to get business loans. Robinson's bank would help black citizens obtain loans and mortgages. Freedom National Bank was dedicated on January 4, 1965. Robinson said it was more than just a bank. It was a chance for black Americans to become part of the country's economy. He said he hoped the success of Freedom National would encourage other banks to be "color blind."[3] The bank did extremely well, and Robinson began speaking out on such issues as poverty and urban development.

He also returned to the world of baseball—this time as a television commentator. ABC-TV Sports hired Robinson as a television commentator for twenty-seven baseball games starting in April 1965. He was paid $500 for each game. Robinson had never lost his interest in

Robinson devoted his energy to civil rights issues, too. Here he joined a picket line to demand more jobs for African Americans.

baseball and often watched the games on television. He had also written two books: *Baseball Has Done It* in 1964 and *Breakthrough to the Big Leagues* in 1965.

One of Robinson's businesses, however, did not get off the ground. Robinson had always been devoted to golf, especially since his retirement from baseball. He hoped to organize a golf club that would welcome both blacks and whites. In Stamford, Connecticut, Robinson was not allowed to join the all-white High Ridge Country Club. He had to play on the public course. Robinson found land for his dream golf course in nearby Lewisboro, New York. A legal battle began when the owners of adjoining land objected and took the case to the State Supreme Court. The court ruled against Robinson, who took the case to the State Commission on Human Rights. Even so, many of the blacks who had planned to invest in the golf course backed down. Frustrated, Robinson gave up as well.

By the late 1960s, problems with Jackie Jr. had grown worse. Robinson's eldest son had fought in the Vietnam War and, like many Vietnam War veterans, returned home a troubled young man. In March 1968, he was arrested for possession of marijuana and heroin, and for carrying a revolver.

The year 1968 held more tragedy. On April 4, civil rights leader Martin Luther King, Jr., was assassinated. Two months later, Senator Robert F. Kennedy was also murdered. Later that year, Robinson received another blow when his mother, Mallie, died at the age of seventy-eight.

Robinson himself was not feeling well. He visited a doctor in June and learned that he had suffered a mild heart attack. His health grew worse, and after an exam the next year, Robinson was told that he had only another couple of years to live. Diabetes was taking its toll on his

Robinson in 1971.

◆ ◆ ◆ ◆ ◆

circulation and his sight, and his body was simply breaking down. He had both heart and lung disease.

In June 1971, Robinson received the worst news of all. Jackie Jr., who had been doing well in a drug rehabilitation program, was killed in a car accident on his way home from New Haven, Connecticut. The family was devastated.

Even though Robinson was crippled by various illnesses, he still made public appearances. He was given honorary degrees at Bethune-Cookman College in Florida as well as a degree from Sacred Heart University in Connecticut. He also attended Old-Timers' Day at Dodger Stadium in Los Angeles on June 4, 1972. There, he saw his Dodger number retired, along with the numbers of Sandy Koufax and Roy Campanella. "This is truly one of the greatest moments of my life," he said.[4] Robinson also kept busy with his autobiography, *I Never Had It Made*. Blind in his right eye and barely able to see out of his left, he worked on the book with writer Alfred Duckett.

On October 24, 1972, worn out physically and emotionally, Robinson suffered a heart attack and died at his home in Stamford, Connecticut. "He was a magnificent man," said Stanley Glenn, a former Negro Leagues player. "But we're only men and no matter how big and

"A LIFE IS NOT IMPORTANT EXCEPT IN THE IMPACT IT HAS ON OTHER LIVES."

Jackie Robinson

Robinson's life more than lived up to the quotation on his gravestone.

tough you think you are, all these things that we do take their toll. That's why at 53, Jackie was no more."[5]

Jackie Robinson will always be remembered as a tremendous athlete, but he was much more than that. He spent most of his life working to gain equality for African Americans. "Jackie put blacks in the mainstream. He was the pioneer, the symbol, that paved the way . . . ," said Lou Brock of the St. Louis Cardinals. "There are times now I mention his name and I get a blank stare from young people. . . . They have to know what went before. They have to learn that Jackie Robinson was responsible in some ways for a lot of what we all have today."[6]

Robinson's life and work live on in the many schools, parks, organizations, and community centers that bear his name. The Jackie Robinson Foundation, registered by Rachel Robinson in 1973, gives grants to minority students so they can attend college. Jackie Robinson was awarded the Presidential Medal of Freedom by President Reagan in 1984. In 1996, President Clinton authorized gold and silver coins to commemorate the fiftieth anniversary of Robinson's major league contract. In 1997, his number—42—was retired for all time. In 2005, he was given a Congressional Gold Medal.

Robinson devoted his life to standing up for what he believed in. "Jackie was a man who would do anything to help one of his own," said Gene Benson, a former Negro Leagues player. "That was his secret, you understand? He went out and gave his life for black athletes."[7]

Chronology

1919—Jack Roosevelt Robinson is born January 31, near Cairo, Georgia.

1920—Family moves to Pasadena, California.

1937—Attends Pasadena Junior College.

1938—Sets national junior college record in broad jump.

1939—Enrolls at University of California at Los Angeles.

1941—Meets future wife, Rachel Isum, at UCLA; works as an athletic director at a National Youth Administration unit is Atascadero, California.

1942—Joins the United States Army and is sent to Fort Riley, Kansas.

1943—Promoted to Second Lieutenant and named morale officer for his African-American unit.

1944—Is court-martialed by the army and found not guilty; is honorable discharged.

1945—Plays for the Kansas City Monarchs in the Negro Leagues; meets Branch Rickey and signs contract with the Dodger organization to play for the Montreal Royals.

1946—Marries Rachel Isum; starts playing for Montreal Royals; son Jackie Jr. is born.

CHRONOLOGY

1947—Starts playing for the Brooklyn Dodgers; is named National League Rookie of the Year.

1949—Becomes one of the first African Americans— along with Roy Campanella, Don Newcombe, and Larry Doby—to play in All-Star Game.

1949—Voted Most Valuable Player in the National League.

1950—Daughter Sharon is born; Robinson stars in the movie *The Jackie Robinson Story*.

1952—Son David is born.

1955—Robinsons move to Stamford, Connecticut; Brooklyn Dodgers win the World Series.

1956—Receives the Spingarn Medal, the highest honor awarded by the National Association for the Advancement of Colored People (NAACP).

1957—Retires from baseball; works for Chock Full o' Nuts; chairs the NAACP Freedom Fund drive.

1960—Campaigns for Richard Nixon for president.

1962—Inducted into the Baseball Hall of Fame.

1964—Helps found the Freedom National Bank.

1972—Dies October 24 at home in Stamford.

1973—Rachel creates the Jackie Robinson Foundation to help African-American students with their education.

1984—Is awarded the Presidential Medal of Freedom.

2005—Is awarded the Congressional Gold Medal.

Chapter Notes

Chapter 1. The Experiment

1. Jules Tygiel, *Baseball's Great Experiment: Jackie Robinson and His Legacy* (New York: Oxford University Press, 1983), p. 54.

2. Jackie Robinson, *I Never Had It Made: An Autobiography* (Hopewell, N.J.: Ecco Press, 1995), p. 28.

3. Roger Kahn, *The Era 1947–1957: When the Yankees, the Giants, and the Dodgers Ruled the World* (New York: Ticknor & Fields, 1993), p. 31.

4. Donald Honig, *Baseball When the Grass Was Real* (New York: Coward, McCann & Geoghegan, Inc., 1975), p. 188.

5. Ibid., p. 186.

6. Geoffrey C. Ward, *Baseball: An Illustrated History* (New York: Alfred A. Knopf, 1994), p. 287.

7. Arnold Rampersad, *Jackie Robinson: A Biography* (New York: Alfred A. Knopf, 1997), p. 126.

8. Ibid.

9. Stanley Cohen, *Dodgers! The First 100 Years* (New York: Carol Publishing Group, 1990), p. 80.

10. Tygiel, p. 66.

11. Robinson, p. 33.

12. "Rickey Takes Slap at Negro Leagues," *The New York Times*, October 23, 1945.

13. Mark Robowsky, *A Complete History of the Negro Leagues: 1884 to 1955* (New York: Carol Publishing Group, 1995), pp. 279–280.

Chapter 2. Growing Up

1. Jackie Robinson, *I Never Had It Made: An Autobiography* (Hopewell, N.J.: Ecco Press, 1995), pp. 4–5.

2. Maury Allen, *Jackie Robinson: A Life Remembered* (New York: Franklin Watts, 1987), p. 21.

3. David Falkner, *Great Time Coming: The Life of Jackie Robinson from Baseball to Birmingham* (New York: Simon and Schuster, 1995), p. 30.

4. Allen, p. 20.

5. Robinson, p. 5.

6. Ibid., p. 6.

7. Rachel Robinson, *Jackie Robinson: An Intimate Portrait* (New York: Harry N. Abrams, Inc., 1996), p. 17.

8. Falkner, p. 32.

9. Ibid.

10. Jackie Robinson, p. 7.

11. Allen, p. 22.

Chapter 3. College

1. David Falkner, *Great Time Coming: The Life of Jackie Robinson from Baseball to Birmingham* (New York: Simon and Schuster, 1995), p. 44.

2. Arnold Rampersad, *Jackie Robinson: A Biography* (New York: Alfred A. Knopf, 1997), p. 55.

3. Ibid., p. 69.

4. Rachel Robinson, *Jackie Robinson: An Intimate Portrait* (New York: Harry N. Abrams, Inc., 1996), p. 22.

5. Jackie Robinson, *I Never Had It Made: An Autobiography* (Hopewell, N.J.: Ecco Press, 1995), p. 11.

Chapter 4. Army Life

1. Arnold Rampersad, *Jackie Robinson: A Biography* (New York: Alfred A. Knopf, 1997), p. 83.

2. Ibid., p. 86.

3. Jules Tygiel, ed., *The Jackie Robinson Reader: Perspectives on an American Hero* (New York: Dutton, 1997), p. 41.

4. Jackie Robinson, *I Never Had It Made: An Autobiography* (Hopewell, N.J.: Ecco Press, 1995), p. 14.

5. David Falkner, *Great Time Coming: The Life of Jackie Robinson from Baseball to Birmingham* (New York: Simon and Schuster, 1995), p. 75.

6. Tygiel, p. 43.

7. Jackie Robinson, p. 18.

Chapter 5. The Negro Leagues

1. Mark Robowsky, *A Complete History of the Negro Leagues: 1884 to 1955* (New York: Carol Publishing Group, 1995), p. xiv.

2. Geoffrey C. Ward, *Baseball: An Illustrated History* (New York: Alfred A. Knopf, 1994), p. 220.

3. Ibid., p. 244.

4. Ibid., p. 245.

5. Jackie Robinson, *I Never Had It Made: An Autobiography* (Hopewell, N.J.: .Ecco Press, 1995), p. 23.

6. *ESPN Classic: Sports Century*, Jackie Robinson Video, 2001.

7. Roger Kahn, *The Era 1947–1957: When the Yankees, the Giants, and the Dodgers Ruled the World* (New York: Ticknor & Fields, 1993), p. 46.

8. Arnold Rampersad, *Jackie Robinson: A Biography* (New York: Alfred A. Knopf, 1997), p. 122.

9. Jules Tygiel, *Baseball's Great Experiment: Jackie Robinson and His Legacy* (New York: Oxford University Press, 1983), p. 71.

10. Ibid., p. 74.

11. "Branch Rickey Praised," *The New York Times*, October 26, 1945.

12. "Rickey Takes Slap at Negro Leagues," *The New York Times*, October 23, 1945.

Chapter 6. The Montreal Royals

1. David Falkner, *Great Time Coming: The Life of Jackie Robinson from Baseball to Birmingham* (New York: Simon and Schuster, 1995), p. 121.

2. Rachel Robinson, *Jackie Robinson: An Intimate Portrait* (New York: Harry N. Abrams, Inc., 1996), p. 43.

3. Ibid., p. 46.

4. Ibid., p. 52.

5. *Time 100: Heroes and Icons*. The Trailblazer: Jackie Robinson. Time, Inc., 2003. <http://www.time.com/time/time100/heroes/profile/robinson01.html> (September 10, 2004).

6. Falkner, p. 139.

7. Arnold Rampersad, *Jackie Robinson: A Biography* (New York: Alfred A. Knopf, 1997), p. 153.

8. *ESPN Classic: Sports Century*, Jackie Robinson Video, 2001.

9. Rampersad, p. 156.

10. Ibid., p. 157.

Chapter 7. Welcome to Brooklyn

1. Roger Kahn, *The Era 1947–1957: When the Yankees, the Giants, and the Dodgers Ruled the World* (New York: Ticknor & Fields, 1993), p. 33.

2. *ESPN Classic: Sports Century*, Jackie Robinson Video, 2001.

3. Kahn, p. 35.

4. Ibid., pp. 35–36.

5. Roscoe McGowen, "Dodgers to Drop 10 Men by Sunday," *The New York Times*, April 1, 1947.

6. Arthur Daley, "Sports of the Times: Opening Day at Ebbets Field," *The New York Times*, April 16, 1947.

7. Ibid.

8. Maury Allen, *Jackie Robinson: A Life Remembered* (New York: Franklin Watts, 1987), p. 113.

9. Geoffrey C. Ward, *Baseball: An Illustrated History* (New York: Alfred A. Knopf, 1994), p. 230.

10. Personal interview, June 18, 2003.

11. Arnold Rampersad, *Jackie Robinson: A Biography* (New York: Alfred A. Knopf, 1997), p. 172.

12. Daley, "Sports of the Times: Opening Day at Ebbets Field."

13. Jackie Robinson, *I Never Had It Made: An Autobiography* (Hopewell, N.J.: Ecco Press, 1995), p. 61.

14. Rampersad, pp. 174–175.

15. Ibid., p. 182.

16. Kahn, p. 35.

Chapter 8. Baseball and Beyond

1. Jackie Robinson, *I Never Had It Made: An Autobiography* (Hopewell, N.J.: Ecco Press, 1995), p 76.

2. Arnold Rampersad, *Jackie Robinson: A Biography* (New York: Alfred A. Knopf, 1997), p. 217.

3. Personal interview, June 18, 2003.

4. Rachel Robinson, *Jackie Robinson: An Intimate Portrait* (New York: Harry N. Abrams, Inc., 1996), p. 113.

Chapter 9. Number 42

1. David Falkner, *Great Time Coming: The Life of Jackie Robinson, from Baseball to Birmingham* (New York: Simon and Schuster, 1995), p. 219.

2. Maury Allen, *Jackie Robinson: A Life Remembered* (New York: Franklin Watts, 1987), p. 118.

3. *Sporting News: Baseball*, Jackie Robinson. <http://www.sportingnews.com/archives/jackie/1956.html> (September 10, 2004).

4. Jules Tygiel, ed., *The Jackie Robinson Reader: Perspectives on an American Hero* (New York: Dutton, 1997), p. 214.

5. Ibid., p. 217.

Chapter 10. The Final Years

1. David Falkner, *Great Time Coming: The Life of Jackie Robinson, from Baseball to Birmingham* (New York: Simon and Schuster, 1995), p. 290.

2. Jules Tygiel, editor, *The Jackie Robinson Reader: Perspectives on an American Hero* (New York: Dutton, 1997), p. 221.

3. Arnold Rampersad, *Jackie Robinson: A Biography* (New York: Alfred A. Knopf, 1997), p. 394.

4. Ibid., p. 456.

5. Personal interview, June 18, 2003.

6. Maury Allen, *Jackie Robinson: A Life Remembered* (New York: Franklin Watts, 1987), pp. 239–240.

7. Falkner, p. 124.

Further Reading

De Marco, Tony. *Jackie Robinson*. Chanhassen, Minn.: Child's World, 2002.

Mara, Wil. *Jackie Robinson*. New York: Children's Press, 2002.

Schaefer, Lola M. *Jackie Robinson*. Mankato, Minn.: Pebble Books, 2003.

Internet Addresses

Baseball Reference. Statistics on Robinson's baseball career.
<http://www.baseball-reference.com/r/robinja02. shtml>

National Baseball Hall of Fame. Brief biography of Robinson.
<http://www.baseballhalloffame.org/hofers_and_ honorees/hofer_bios/robinson_jackie.htm>

The Sporting News. A large photo gallery and timeline of Robinson's life.
<http://www.sportingnews.com/archives/jackie/index. html>

Index

Page numbers for photographs are in **boldface** type.